Understanding
& Using
TAROT

Provides the student with all the knowledge needed to use this
fascinating and highly accurate divinatory tool properly.

Understanding
& Using
TAROT

Emily Peach

Sterling Publishing Co., Inc.
New York

7   9   10   8

Published in 1990 by Sterling Publishing Company, Inc.
387 Park Avenue South, New York, N.Y. 10016
Originally published in Great Britain by The Aquarian Press
© 1984 by Emily Peach
Distributed in Canada by Sterling Publishing
% Canadian Manda Group, P.O. Box 920, Station U
Toronto, Ontario, Canada M8Z 5P9
Manufactured in the United States of America
All rights reserved

ISBN 0-8069-7194-0

Acknowledgements

My thanks are due to Mrs Dolores Ashcroft-Nowicki who has taught, listened, and advised, and who has generously provided — directly or indirectly — many of the exercises herein; and to Lieutenant Edouard J. Faivre, who patiently and conscientiously read and followed instructions in his role of guinea-pig for the concept of this book. Thank you.

To D.A.N. with love

Contents

Part One:
The Tarot as a Divinatory Tool

1.

Getting Started

Before you begin to tackle any subject, it is as well to collect together the various things you will need to carry it through to the end. Listed below in order of priority are the items you will need to work your way through the first part of this book satisfactorily, and a short explanation of their uses. All of these items are traditionally associated with Tarot cards, but you should not feel bound to follow any of the instructions regarding their design or construction absolutely to the letter. The Tarot is a living tradition; imaginative interpretation of the rules pertaining to it is therefore what is required, rather than a rigid adherence to convention.

1. A Tarot Deck

Nowadays there are a good many different Decks to choose from, and if you grow into a serious student of the Tarot, you will doubtless eventually own more than one of them. When buying your first working Deck, however, it is best to choose the one that most appeals to you *from among those Decks that carry traditional symbolism simply presented*. This is most important. When you are more familiar with the Tarot, you will be able to work comfortably with any Deck, but at the beginning of your career it is better to stay away from exotic Decks and stick with the tried and true. Although it is not nearly so attractive as some of the other available Decks, the Rider-Waite version of the Tarot is probably the best Deck to start work on, and has the added advantage of being very easy to obtain.

2. A Silk Scarf

Traditionally, Tarot cards are kept wrapped in a silk scarf when not in use, and ideally you should have such a scarf ready when you bring your first Tarot deck home with you.

All physical objects collect 'impressions' or 'vibrations' from their surroundings and Tarot cards are no exception. Some people are able to 'read' these impressions, and give an accurate rendering of past events from inanimate objects, but while this is interesting, it is not always desirable. Silk is a fabric that for some reason rejects such 'impressions', and the purpose of the scarf is to keep your cards clean of 'vibrations' that might otherwise adversely affect the quality or accuracy of your readings and meditations. As it is a tradition in the occult that all tools should be hand-made, it would be a good idea to buy some silk (a piece about a foot square will do nicely) and make the scarf yourself.

3. A Wooden Box

When the cards have been wrapped in silk, they should be kept in a wooden box. This box serves very much the same purpose as the scarf, and wood is chosen as the material for much the same reasons as silk is the preferred substance for the scarf. It further protects the cards from adverse 'vibrations' and at the same time preserves them from prying eyes and fingers, and physical wear and tear or accident — spilled coffee for instance, or water from a vase overturned by the family cat.

Again, ideally the box should be made by you, but as very few people have the necessary carpentry skills, it is permissible to buy one. When buying your box, however, please make sure that it is large enough for both cards and scarf to fit inside it comfortably. It is obviously not a good idea to buy a box an eighth of an inch or so too small, and then bend the cards to fit it.

4. A Tarot Cloth

The Tarot cloth is another piece of silk, usually a yard or more square, and fringed. It is used to cover the surface on which you intend to lay out the cards for meditation or reading, and as it is of little use to wrap and box the cards and then lay them out on a surface that may be sticky as well as generally unsuitable, you should make the effort to own one.

If you are at all handy with a needle, and enjoy needle-work, this is an item you can really go to town on, since it should be decorative as well as practical. The material should be black, and of a heavier quality than that used for the scarf. Decoration should be appropriate — the symbol of the Tarot shown opposite is perfect for the purpose — and when you have finished embroidering the design you should fringe the cloth on all four sides. Silk, however heavy, has a tendency to slide, and the fringe will help to weight the cloth and prevent entire readings from ending up in your lap or on the floor.

Obviously, making the Tarot cloth is quite a project, and one that should not be completed hurriedly or carelessly. To begin with therefore it is a good idea to kill two birds with one stone and buy a very large silk scarf to do double duty as both scarf and cloth until such time as you can get around to making the real things properly. When you *have* made the real things, please resist what seems to be a universal temptation to wear them rather than work from them. The cloth doubtless looks both elegant and impressive when draped about the head and shoulders of the reader, but this is not what it is for; its real place is on the table, not on you.

When you have collected together all of the above items, you will be ready to start 'breaking in' your Deck — for a Tarot Deck has to be 'broken in' just like a new pair of shoes. For the first month or so after getting your Deck, you should carry it with you everywhere (*sans* box of course) and sleep with it under your pillow. You should also handle it as much as you possibly can. This will serve to 'activate' you to your Deck, and vice versa; and if you are new to the Tarot, it will help you become accustomed to and familiar with the design and feel of your cards.

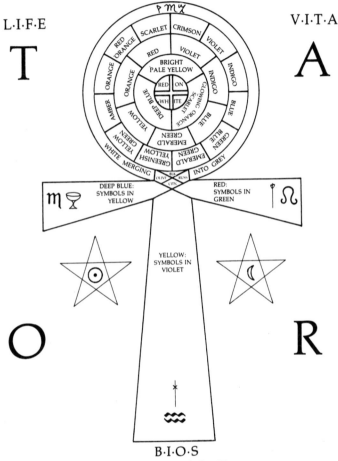

The Symbol of the Tarot

Never let anyone else handle your Deck. It is very personal to you despite the fact that many thousands of people own one just like it. If your friends want to handle and examine Tarot cards (and they will, if they see you handling and examining yours!) then they must buy a Deck of their own. You must not allow them to satisfy their curiosity with your Deck, as this will undo all the good work of 'activation' you have begun, and totally negate the protective qualities of your scarf and box.

2.

Using this Book to your Best Advantage

Having made a capital investment in this book, you would doubtless like to get your money's worth out of it. The best way to do that is to use the book as it was designed and intended to be used; which means going through it chapter by chapter in the correct numerical progression to the very end, with no digressions, short cuts or sneak previews.

This book is designed to enable you to read and use Tarot cards properly as quickly as is humanly possible. Each chapter of it consists of a body of information followed by a test or practice session to enable you to see how well you have absorbed that information. You should get through these chapters at the rate of one per week *at the very most*. Half a chapter a week is fine; three chapters a week is a disaster waiting to happen.

To deal with each chapter successfully, you will need a working knowledge of any information already given you, your Tarot cards, a notebook, a pen, and your common sense. The reading and writing part of each chapter should take up one and a half hours of your time *and no more*. During the rest of your allotted week, you should have the odd half an hour or so of practice and revision per day. Try not to exceed the one and a half hour time limit on the reading and writing sessions, and try not to let your practice sessions run much over an hour and a half either; ninety minutes has been determined to be the learning intake limit at one sitting for the average person, and anything over that will give you mental indigestion and get you no further forward. For the same reason, you should not attempt to gobble up four or five chapters at one sitting, or on four or five consecutive days.

The simplest way to learn anything is to use a 'look, listen and write' process — the very process you used all through your school life. Studying alone is never easy, so if you have a friend or a group of friends interested enough to want to learn with you, then make each chapter a semi-social occasion. Make sure, however, that your friends really do want to learn. One cannot press-gang one's fellow man headlong into the occult, kicking and screaming all the way.

If you do manage to make up a 'learning circle' you should have a different person each week read the chapter aloud, while the rest of you take notes. Make sure that each person is keeping up; the pace of your little class should be the pace of the slowest learner in it. You will find that you will all benefit greatly from the feedback that is generated by this classroom-type situation, and of course it is much easier to practise reading the Tarot if you have someone handy to practise on. Do not, however, elect yourself 'teacher/reader' for the duration, or allow anyone else to do so. All too often the 'teacher/reader' is too busy teaching to learn anything.

If you are learning alone, you can and should follow the 'look, listen and write' process as closely as possible. It is fairly easy to simulate the ideal classroom situation by recording the chapter on a cassette recorder and then playing it back to yourself while you write.

Whether you learn alone or in a group, always make sure that you have the appropriate card in front of you while you work, so that you can examine it and its divinatory meanings at one and the same time, thus relating the two things permanently together. You will notice that on each of the pages dealing with divinatory meanings in this book there is an oblong card-shaped blank space. This blank space serves as a place to put your card while you are working with it.

The meanings in this book are highly simplified, but perfectly adequate. When you have learned them all so thoroughly that you never have to look any of them up, and every one of them springs effortlessly to mind when you glance at the appropriate card, it will be time to read and assimilate as many of the other published meanings as you possibly can. Until that day dawns, however, it would be best *not* to begin on an intensive course of extracurricular reading, as this might result in confusion.

Before you make a start on any chapter dealing with divinatory meanings, always separate the appropriate cards from the rest of the Deck, laying the ones you will be using out on your silk scarf, and packing the rest away in your wooden box. When you are dealing with the Minor Arcana, you should lay out the fourteen cards of the appropriate Suit, beginning with the Ace on the left, and ending Page, Knight, Queen, King on the right. As you deal with each specific card, move it out of its place in line and into a central spot where you can see it clearly, or onto the card-sized blank space in the book. If the card you are examining is supposed to be upside down, make sure it *is* upside down; but above all make sure it is the *right card*. When you are a beginner, and unfamiliar with the cards, it is only too easy to make mistakes.

You may find when you first begin to practise with your cards that although you absorb the meanings of each card quickly and easily, it is difficult to relate one card to another. For this reason you are asked to construct 'fantasy plays' as you work through the chapters dealing with divinatory meanings. Fantasy plays are built by relating the given meaning of one card to the given meaning of another and *making up a story*, and you should begin the fantasy play process directly you have written down the meanings of the first two cards dealt with by any given chapter. When you have gone through every possible combination of those two cards, you should write down the meaning of the next card, and begin the process all over again, constantly changing the position of the cards as you work.

Of necessity, your fantasy plays will be very short in the beginning, but as Suit after Suit becomes available to you, you will find that you are able to make up interesting and involved little histories — particularly if you make good use of the personalities represented by the Court Cards. Do not allow yourself to feel foolish as you go through this process. Fantasy plays are a vitally important part of your learning process; they tend to make the meanings stick in your mind more easily, and set your subconscious mind working for you, besides being great fun to do.

At the end of this chapter you will find a page headed 'Readers Check List — for use with Chapters 1 through 6'. On the reverse side of that page is another check list headed 'Readers Check List — Chapters 7 to End'. You should either mark that page with a paperclip, or tear it out and pin it up in a prominent position near your working area so that you may go over it carefully before you commence your Practice Spreads. The 'Check List' is a list of things you will be doing at the start of every serious reading, and will help you to make doing the right things habitual.

Above all, learn your basics well. Skip nothing and ignore nothing. Make the rules you will be learning and the simplified meanings second nature. Learn the terminology of the field, and use it. You will never regret time expended now, for it will save you countless frustrating hours in the future.

Reader's Check List — For Use with Chapters 1 through 6

1. Read the instructions for the Spread very carefully, and then turn back to this page and complete the Check List.

2. Lay out your silk scarf and Tarot cloth over the surface on which you intend to read.

3. Shuffle the cards you will be using *yourself.*

4. Enquire as to your Querent's Astrological or birth sign, and choose a Significator based on that information.

5. Place the Significator in a central position on the table. Take care to replace any cards you will not be using for the purposes of this Spread back in your wooden box.

6. Hand the cards you will be using for this reading to the Querent, and ask him or her to shuffle the cards while concentrating on the question he or she would like answered. Always ensure that the question asked is in line with the suit or suits you will be using, and that the question is phrased as per any instructions given in the instructions for the Spread.

7. Should the Querent chatter while shuffling, then he or she is obviously not concentrating on the matter at hand. You should politely draw this to your Querent's attention, explaining that the reading may be improperly focused or muddled as a result of this lack of attention, and that the shuffling process must be recommenced from the beginning — in silence.

8. When your Querent has finished shuffling the cards, ask him or her to lay them down on the reading surface, face down and *en bloc*, and then have him or her cut them in half once to the left.

9. Place the *right*-hand pile of the two piles thus created on top of the left-hand pile *yourself*, and then deal with cards, *from the top of the Deck*, in the pattern set out on the page directly following the Instructions for the Spread.

   Always deal the cards from the top of the Deck, and as the Deck was Dignified to your Querent. *Never* 'flip' the cards as you deal them, as this will alter their Dignity. The cards should be turned over as you would turn over the pages of a book.

You are now ready to commence the reading as set forth in the instructions for the Spread.

Reader's Check List — Chapters 7 to End

1.   Read the instructions for the Spread, and then turn back to this page and complete the Check List.

2.   Lay out your silk scarf or Tarot cloth as usual.

3.   Shuffle the cards you will be using yourself.

4.   Decide whether you will be reading for an absent Querent or otherwise.

5.   If you are not reading for an absent Querent, enquire as to your Querent's Astrological or birth sign as usual and choose a Significator based on that information; if you are reading for an absent Querent, decide upon a Significator using your Querent's physical characteristics as guidelines.

6.   Check in the instructions for the Spread as to what, if anything, you are to do with the Significator you have chosen.

7.   Ask your Querent to shuffle and cut in the usual way. If your Querent is not present, perform these actions yourself.

8.   Ensure that your Querent, if present, is concentrating. If he is not present, ensure that you are visualizing correctly and concentrating yourself.

9.   Deal the cards from the top of the Deck in the pattern shown on the page directly following the instructions for the Spread.

10.   Make sure that you handle the cards correctly as you lay them out so as not to alter their Dignity.

11.   Examine the Spread for Majorities, and decide upon the subject of the Spread from that information. Make sure to check for a Subsidiary Majority to ground your reading, and do not make any comment until you have worked out the 'story line' of the Spread in your mind.

You are now ready to commence the practice reading as set forth in the instructions for the Spread.

3.

An Introduction to the Minor Arcana

The seventy-eight cards of the Tarot Deck are divided into two separate units, the **Major Arcana** and the **Minor Arcana**. The Minor Arcana makes up the larger part of the Deck, and consists of fifty-six cards, fifty-two of which correspond to a regular deck of playing cards. The four extra cards are the four **Pages**, which are sometimes called **Knaves** or **Princesses**. The four Pages, along with the **Knights**, **Queens** and **Kings**, are usually called **Court Cards**. Court cards represent *people*. The other cards, or those numbered One through Ten, are called **Small Cards**. Small cards represent *situations* or *events*.

Each card has two separate and distinct meanings for the purposes of **Divination**, which is the word used for the process of reading (or divining from) the cards. When the design or picture on the card shows the card to be **Upright**, it is referred to as being **Dignified**. Dignified cards show *positive*, *helpful* aspects. When the design or picture on the card shows the card to be **Upside-Down,** or reversed, it is referred to as being **Ill-Dignified**. Ill-Dignified cards show *negative, unhelpful* aspects. You should always read the cards as being Dignified or Ill-dignified to you the reader, and *not* to the person you are reading for. As cards are always read according to Dignity, you should obviously never go through your Deck making sure that all the cards are the same way up before you begin, as this will result in a garbled and inaccurate reading.

Like a regular playing card deck, the Minor Arcana is divided into four **Suits**. Several different names have at one time or another been assigned to these Suits, but for the purposes of this book, they will be called **Wands**, **Cups**, **Swords** and **Pentacles**. If your particular Deck does not bear these names, it would be as well to go through this book and write in the alternative titles wherever they appear.

Each Suit represents:

1. One of the Four Aristotelian Elements, that is to say either Fire, Water, Air or Earth

2. An Aspect of our Daily Lives
3. Three of the Twelve Signs of the Zodiac
4. One of the Four Letters of the Tetragrammaton. The Tetragrammaton is the Divine Name, and is made up of four Hebrew letters, Yod, Heh, Vau and Heh Final, or Yahweh

Thus, the Suit of Wands represents:

1. The Element of Fire
2. The Career Aspect of our Daily Lives
3. The Three Fiery Signs of the Zodiac, or Leo, Aries and Sagittarius
4. Yod, or Primal Energy

The table below sets out these attributions fully as they apply to all four Suits.

It is primarily from the Astrological or Zodiacal attributions that one chooses, at the commencement of each reading, a **Significator**, which is the term used for the card chosen to represent the **Querent**, or the person for whom one is reading.

Significators are always chosen from among the sixteen available Court Cards. In practice, this means that there are three possible alternatives to choose from if the Querent is a man, and two if the Querent is a woman. These alternatives occur because some attention must also be paid to the probable age of the Querent when choosing a Significator. Usually:

Pages represent children or virgins.
Knights represent young men under the age of thirty.
Queens represent married or sexually mature women.
Kings represent mature men.

Suit Name	Element	Astrological Signs	Aspect of our Daily Lives	Letter of the Tetragrammaton
Wands	Fire	Leo Aries Sagittarius	Career	Yod Primal Energy
Cups	Water	Pisces Cancer Scorpio	Emotion	Heh Emergence of Energy into Form
Swords	Air	Gemini Libra Aquarius	Mental	Vau Stabilization of Form
Pentacles	Earth	Taurus Capricorn Virgo	Money and Material	Heh [final] Completion of Energy into Form

Thus, a man over the age of thirty, and born under the Astrological sign Aries, would take the King of Wands as his Significator; a married woman born under the sign of Cancer would take the Queen of Cups as her Significator, and so on.

Because the choice of Significator rests so heavily upon the Querent's Astrological sign, it would be as well to learn the correct dates applicable to each sign, for even in this Astrologically oriented day and age, there are still some people who do not know their Astrological or birth sign, and if you do not know it either, you could find yourself considerably embarrassed. A table showing these dates appears on page 22. As to the age and possible sexual experience of your Querent, you must of course use your discretion and common sense. It is never acceptable to make enquiry as to either point!

One further set of attributions completes those applicable to the Minor Arcana. This set of attributions relates one of the four Elements to each of the four Court Cards of each Suit, as follows:

All **Pages** are attributed to the Element of **Earth**.
All **Knights** are attributed to the Element of **Fire**.
All **Queens** are attributed to the Element of **Water**.
All **Kings** are attributed to the Element of **Air**.

Using these attributions, it is possible to 'name' the Court Cards, i.e., the Knight of Wands becomes Fire of Fire, since he is both a Knight and a Wand; the Page of Wands becomes Earth of Fire, and so on. The table below sets out these attributions as they apply to all of the Court Cards.

The Elemental 'Names' of the Court Cards		
Wands	Page Knight Queen King	Earth of Fire Fire of Fire Water of Fire Air of Fire
Cups	Page Knight Queen King	Earth of Water Fire of Water Water of Water Air of Water
Swords	Page Knight Queen King	Earth of Air Fire of Air Water of Air Air of Air
Pentacles	Page Knight Queen King	Earth of Earth Fire of Earth Water of Earth Air of Earth

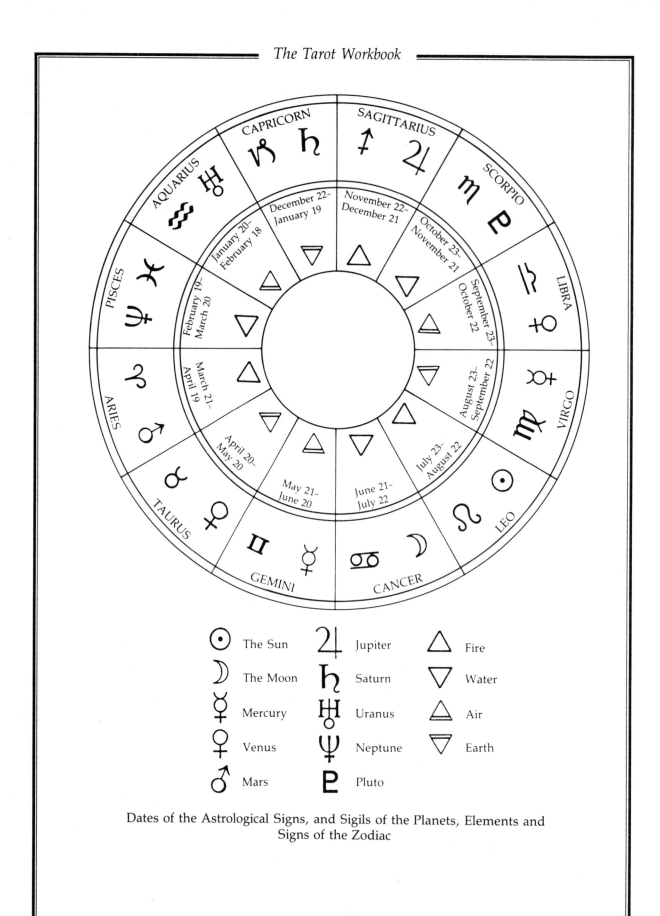

Dates of the Astrological Signs, and Sigils of the Planets, Elements and Signs of the Zodiac

Besides their various other attributions, each card of the Tarot Deck is assigned a simple numerical value. These numbers have nothing to do with the various other numbers that will be assigned to various parts of the Deck later, but are used only to count the cards in complicated **Spreads** or **Layouts**. The words 'Spread' and 'Layout' are used in the Tarot to denote the various patterns in which the cards are laid out to be read.

For counting purposes only, therefore, the cards of the Minor Arcana take their numerical values as follows:

Small cards numbered Two through Ten, take the face value of the card for their numerical value. Thus, The Seven of Swords will take the value of Seven, the Two of Cups the value of Two, and so on.

Aces are not considered to be Small cards for counting purposes, and take the value of Five. (*Not* one, *not* ten and *not* eleven as Aces sometimes do in various card games.)

Three of the four sets of Court cards, the Knights, Queens and Kings, all take the value of Four.

Pages take the value of Seven.

Naturally you will not be using all of these attributions and numerical values immediately, or even in the near future. Nevertheless, and despite the fact that they will be repeated at least once hereafter, you should try to learn them *now*, however arbitrary and useless they appear to be. Indeed, I would strongly recommend that you do not go on to the next chapter until you have fully assimilated this one, tables and all. There is a vast body of information associated with the Tarot, and these basic attributions (and a lot more of them that you have not seen as yet) are the foundation stones on which your knowledge and understanding of the subject will stand — or fall. They are also cumulative in nature; if you fail to absorb them piecemeal as they are given, or consistently persist in skipping over them to get at more interesting things, you will one day arrive at point *non plus* and have to come back to them in order to go on — at which point by the law that governs such things they will appear to be three times more difficult and confusing than they really are.

I am well aware (for I went through it myself) that learning these attributions and numerical values and the Astrological attributions and their relative dates is laborious, unromantic and boring. You should consider, however, before you consign them all to limbo as quite useless that most of the well-established and more useful Spreads depend absolutely upon the simple process of splitting the Deck, *finding the Significator*, and reading only that portion of the Deck which contains it. Since the mere fact of splitting the Deck reduces the number of *immediate* variables from seventy-eight to less than seventy-eight, thus narrowing the field of operations to a much more manageable level, this is obviously a very useful little device indeed. It is a device, however, that *you* will never be able to take advantage of unless you learn how to choose a Significator competently in the first place.

To help you get used to the attributions and the many new terms used in this chapter, several blank Charts and a questionnaire appear on the following pages. When you can fill them all in with an accuracy of about 95 per cent you will be ready — and able — to go on to the next chapter with no fear of having to read this one all over again.

Questionnaire

1. How many cards make up the Tarot Deck?......................................
2. How many cards make up the Major Arcana?...............................
3. How many cards make up the Minor Arcana?..............................
4. There are four Suits in the Minor Arcana. What are the names of the four Suits?

      i)   ....
      ii)   ....
      iii)   ....
      iv)   ....

5. How many cards are there in each Suit?...................................
6. There are four Court Cards in each Suit. What are the names of these four cards?

      i)   ....
      ii)   ....
      iii)   ....
      iv)   ....

7. Every card in the Minor Arcana has a simple numerical value that is used for counting purposes only. What is the simple numerical value of the following cards?

      i)   The Ace of Wands...
      ii)   The Two of Cups..
      iii) The Knight of Pentacles...
      iv) The Page of Swords..

8. The cards numbered 1 through 10 of each suit have a specific name. What is it?...
9. Some of the cards of the Minor Arcana have 'Elemental Names'. What is the name of these cards?..
10. There is a specific way of finding the card called the 'Significator'. What is it?...
11. Your Querent does not know his Astrological sign. His birth date is 4 August 1946. What is:

      i)   His Astrological sign?...
      ii)   His Significator?..

Suit Name	Element	Astrological Signs	Aspect of our Daily Lives	Letter of the Tetragrammaton
Wands				
Cups				
Swords				
Pentacles				

The Elemental 'Names' of the Court Cards		
Wands	Page Knight Queen King	
Cups	Page Knight Queen King	
Swords	Page Knight Queen King	
Pentacles	Page Knight Queen King	

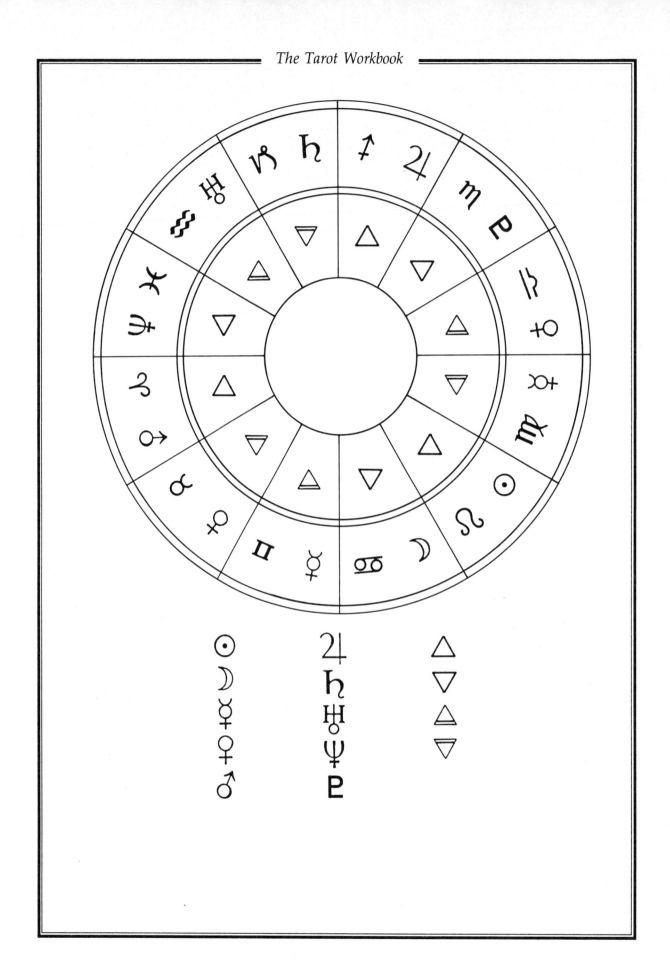

4.

The Suit of Wands

As you will recall, for the purposes of divination the Suits of Wands represents:

1. The Career aspect of our Daily Lives
2. The Element of Fire
3. The Three Fiery Signs of the Zodiac — Leo, Aries and Sagittarius
4. The letter Yod [primal energy] of the Tetragrammaton

In practice, this means that if a majority of the Suit of Wands, or more cards of that Suit than any other, should appear in a Spread, then the Spread will relate to matters of career, work and business.

You must beware of associating this Suit with money, or material gain. A wonderful business opportunity, for instance, does not automatically guarantee a financial increase, and you should always look to the Suit of Pentacles to forecast the financial side of any business transaction indicated by the cards of the Suit of Wands. Thus, a complete absence of Pentacles in a Spread containing a majority of the Suit of Wands could well indicate some charitable work in which the Querent is heavily involved, but for which he receives no monetary reward, or a project that he has just begun that has brought in no money to date.

You should always bear in mind too that your Querent may not be engaged in what is usually termed 'gainful employment', in which case a majority of the Suit of Wands may be forecasting a new venture that will change his circumstances, or a hobby or project on which he spends a great deal of time and which could be turned to good account if he so wished.

Because of the fiery nature of this Suit, a majority of it will always forecast great energy and force; a hectically busy time and the possibility of many new projects.

Naturally, the Court Cards of this Suit will be chosen to represent persons who have Aries, Leo or Sagittarius as their Astrological or birth sign. On some occasions, however, it may prove impossible to discover exactly what the relevant birth sign of a particular individual may be. This tends to occur when the Querent enquires about a friend or relative who is not present and whose birthday he does not know or cannot remember. If this should prove to be the case, a Significator may be chosen using the subject's physical colouring as a guideline. On occasions like this, of course, it is also permissible to enquire as to the subject's age, so as to be sure of making the right choice from among the available Court Cards.

The physical characteristics appropriate to the Suit of Wands are as follows:

	Hair Colour	Eye Colour
Page	Red or Blond	Blue
Knight	Blond	Blue or Grey
Queen	Red or Blond	Blue or Brown
King	Red or Blond	Grey or Hazel

These attributions form a much less definite and satisfactory basis for choice of Significator than do the Astrological signs, but are nevertheless worth committing to memory so as to be available for use should the circumstances arise.

Before you go on to deal with divinatory meanings of this Suit, please make sure that you have all fourteen cards of the Suit laid out on the table before you in the order described in Chapter 3 and that the other cards of your Deck are packed safely away in your wooden box. Check each card on the table carefully to make sure that it is indeed a Wand and not a Sword, and that the Court Cards are Court Cards and not Major Arcana cards, and moreover that they are the *right* Court Cards. Remember that when you have written down the Dignified and Ill-Dignified meanings of the Ace and Two of Wands you should immediately commence your first fantasy play, and that you should continue with these fantasy plays card by card until you arrive at the King of Wands. As you deal with each card, try to ensure that you can see it clearly as you write; and take the time to examine it carefully. If you cannot close your eyes and see it with comparative clarity as to colour and content in your mind's eye, then you have not examined it carefully enough, and should keep looking at it until you *can* see it in your mind's eye. Remember too that when you are writing down the Ill-Dignified meaning of any card, then the card itself should not be sitting looking at you Dignified while you are doing it, but should be Ill-Dignified as well.

When you have finished writing down all the meanings, and completed your last fantasy play, go on *without delay* to the Reader's Check List and the Practice Spread. Remember that you will be using only the Suit of Wands for the purposes of this Spread, so you should ensure that your Querent concentrates on his or her career rather than some other aspect of life.

The listening, the writing, the careful examination of the cards and above all the fantasy plays have primed you to perform very well on the Practice

Spread, so please don't sit down and have a cup of tea and a chat before you start it! There will be plenty of time — and a much greater need — for relaxation and refreshment when you have completed the chapter and packed everything away until the next time.

The Ace of Wands

The Root of the Powers of Fire

Numerical Value: 5
Season: Spring
Direction: South

Dignified: Aggression, innovation, inventiveness. New beginnings, new enterprises, aggressively pursued. Artistic inspiration. Fertility. Conception. Virility.

Ill-Dignified: False starts. Projects conceived but not pursued. Impotence. Barrenness. Sterility. In a woman's spread, problems with men.

Note: The Aces of each Suit always relate to new beginnings, and, as you can see from the notes above, can be used as *timing* and *direction* cards. If the card is ill-dignified, of course, the timing will become 'late Spring', and the direction 'further South', the presupposition being of a greater lapse of time or distance.

The Two of Wands

The Lord of Dominion

Numerical Value: 2

Dignified: Earned success. Authority and wealth gained by hard work. Projects brought to fruition by strength of will. Prosperity; ownership and job-related benefits (i.e., a company car, a life assurance policy, etc.)

Ill-Dignified: Pride and ambition. The will to power. Wealth and authority gained by or used for improper or dishonest means.

The Three of Wands

The Lord of Established Strength

Numerical Value: 3

Dignified: Opportunity. Successful trade or commerce. Success arising from the practical help and collaboration of a partner or mentor — *or circumstance*, i.e., the fact of being in the right place at the right time.

Ill-Dignified: Disappointment in a venture that looked promising, but has failed. Refusal of assistance offered through pride or arrogance. Obstinacy.

The Four of Wands

The Lord of Perfected Work

Numerical Value: 4

Dignified: Triumphant completion of a project. Prosperity and celebration. Peace and harmony. The possibility of a romance, depending upon surrounding cards.

Ill-Dignified: Obstacles and completion delayed, but imminent. A period of rest and peace. A hiatus period before the successful conclusion of a matter, or a quiet period before great activity.

The Five of Wands

The Lord of Strife

Numerical Value: 5

Dignified: Strife, trouble, tests, competition, opposition. Success can only be gained through strenuous and unrelenting hard work.

Ill-Dignified: Legal disputes that could be avoided. Acrimonious discussion and spite. A person who indulges in compulsive and unnecessary competition with others.

The Six of Wands

The Lord of Victory

Numerical Value: 6

Dignified:	Triumph. Victory after strife or effort. Success through hard labour. Good news and advancement as a result of previous work.
Ill-Dignified:	Delayed rewards. Delayed or bad news. Red tape. Fear of a victorious rival. Disappointment due to the advancement of a rival over oneself.

The Seven of Wands

The Lord of Valour

Numerical Value: 7

Dignified: Obstacles and powerful opposition which must be faced or losses will be incurred. Slight success after hard work, and the promise of success thereafter. Courage and steadfastness in the face of adversity.

Ill-Dignified: Indecision or timidity rooted in previous negative experiences that results in lost opportunities. A person who has given up in the face of opposition, when in fact the end was in sight.

Note: This card may denote a deliberate refusal of success, a turning away from success through fear of responsibility, dependent, of course, upon surrounding cards.

The Eight of Wands

The Lord of Swiftness

Numerical Value: 8

Dignified: Swift action over short periods of time. An end to delay. News, communications, telephone calls and letters. Perhaps journeys. Hope of change for the better.

Ill-Dignified: Impetuous and foolhardy action. Embezzlement or theft. Bad news or dismissal from employment. Journeys delayed or cancelled unexpectedly.

The Nine of Wands

The Lord of Great Strength

Numerical Value: 9

Dignified: Productivity, strength, good health and stability. An unassailable and secure position in life. Victory assured against possible opposition.

Ill-Dignified: Impractical and unproductive schemes. An inability to compromise leading to defence of untenable positions. Obstinacy. Weakness of character. Possible ill health. The crumbling of an apparently secure position, or loss of tenure.

The Ten of Wands

The Lord of Oppression

Numerical Value: 10

Dignified: The price of success. Great good fortune and its attendant demands on time. The growth of a business or hobby beyond the capacity of its creator to manage it alone while pursuing a satisfactory social life. Excessive overtime in a job.

Ill-Dignified: Selfish spoiling of the pleasures of others through envy. Deceit and lies. The unnecessary burdening of oneself with tasks that could and should best be delegated to others.

The Page of Wands

The Princess of the Shining Flame; The Rose of the Palace of Fire

Numerical Value: 7
Elemental Name: Earth of
              Fire

Dignified:	A resourceful and ambitious person who has great enthusiasm and vigour. A person who is quick to respond emotionally; either with love or anger. Depending upon surrounding cards (i.e., the Eight of Wands) a messenger bringing exciting and stimulating news.
Ill-Dignified:	A domineering and superficial person who wants to achieve much by the shortest possible route and so can be untrustworthy and deceitful. Depending upon surrounding cards, the bearer of bad or disappointing news.

Note: The appearance of a Knave almost always signifies change (in the case of the Suit of Wands, a change of career or job) for better or worse, according to dignity.

Postulate the Eight of Wands Ill-Dignified (dismissal) and the Knave of Wands appearing together in a Spread to illustrate how the cards can reinforce a message to the reader.

The Knight of Wands

The Lord of the Flame and the Lightning; The King of the Spirits of Fire

Numerical Value: 4
Elemental Name: Fire of
Fire

Dignified: An unpredictable or impetuous person, who is swift to act and enjoys action. Depending on surrounding cards, this card may signify sudden departures, hasty decisions, or change of residence.

Ill-Dignified: A narrow minded and contentious person, a bigot, and a lover of discord for its own sake. Depending upon surrounding cards, journeys delayed, a procrastinator.

Note: As you can see above, Court Cards do not always represent people. The Knight of Wands Dignified in close proximity with any card signifying travelling or change of residence will be reinforcing that card, and will not signify a person.

The Queen of Wands

The Queen of the Thrones of Flame

Numerical Value: 4
Elemental Name: Water
of Fire

Dignified: A generous woman, practical and kind, and capable of independent thought and action, but home loving. A country-woman. Depending upon surrounding cards, the success of a venture.

Ill-Dignified: A jealous and domineering woman, obstinate and tending to imagine wrongs. A woman who allows her loved ones no independence or resorts to emotional blackmail.

The King of Wands

The Prince of the Chariot of Fire

Numerical Value: 4
Elemental Name: Air of
                Fire

Dignified: An honest and conscientious person, loyal and generous, loving traditional ways and family life. A just and enterprising man of authority. Dependent upon surrounding cards, a mediator or arbitrator.

Ill-Dignified: An autocratic and intolerant person, prejudiced, ruthless, and lacking in feeling for others.

Instructions for the 'Yes or No' Simple Answering Spread

This Spread is designed to give a definite answer to a definite question, so you must take care to have your Querent phrase his question in such a way that it can be satisfactorily answered by a simple 'yes' or 'no'. Questions beginning 'When will I...' are therefore unacceptable for the purposes of this particular Spread, although another 'Yes or No' Spread you will be given later will answer such questions perfectly adequately.

For the purposes of illustration, we will assume that the question was: 'Will I get a substantial salary raise in June?'

Card number One, which overlays the Significator, is the pivot card which provides the 'yes' or 'no' answer for this Spread. If Card number One is Dignified, then the answer to the question is Yes. If it is Ill-Dignified, then the answer is No. Card number One is therefore obviously the first card to be read.

Cards numbered Two and Three should next be read. These cards are labelled 'Helpful influences' on the diagram, but you should beware of interpreting these cards as *helpful to the Querent*, because this is not so. They are helpful influences *to the answer received*. If the answer to our question was 'no', these cards will therefore tell you *why* no substantial salary raise was received in June and *not* what will help the Querent to obtain such a salary increase in the future.

Cards numbered Six and Seven come next. These cards are labelled 'Adverse influences'. Again, you should remember that these cards are not *adverse to the Querent, but only adverse to the answer*. If the answer was again 'no', like the example above, these cards will show *what would have helped* the Querent to obtain the raise he wanted.

Cards numbered Four and Five show what the Querent *thought* about the circumstances.

Cards numbered Eight and Nine show what the Querent *felt* about the circumstances.

These two latter sets of cards are very often extraordinarily at odds with each other, but you should not be concerned about this. It is very common to be, say, disappointed about not getting a much needed raise and still remain quite happy about the job situation as a whole.

When you have read *all* the cards through once in this way, you should return to card number One and read this again *upon its own merits*. This card can then be used as the 'outcome card' for the entire reading.

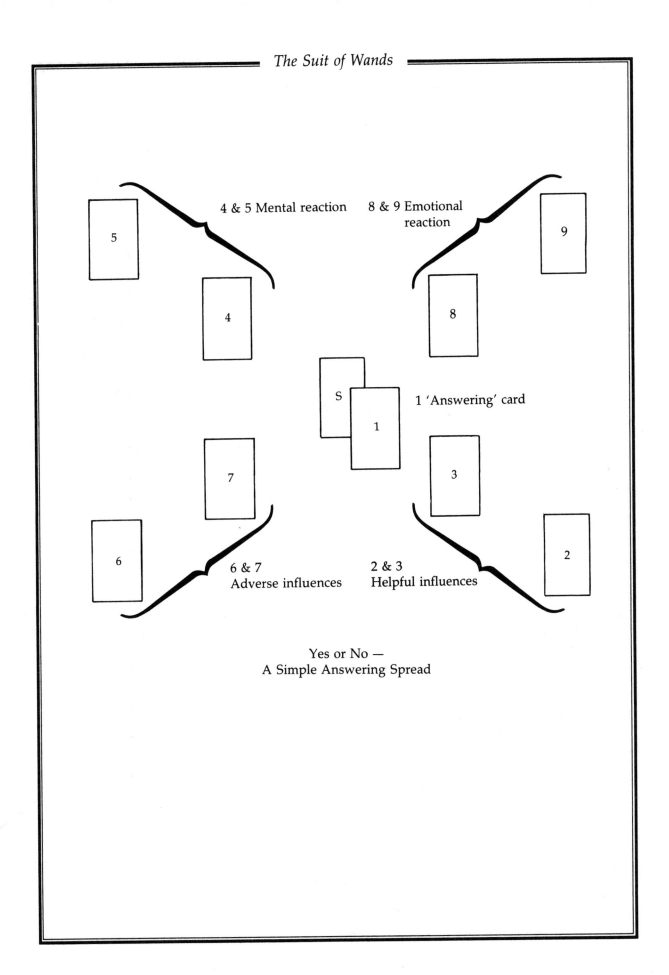

4 & 5 Mental reaction

8 & 9 Emotional reaction

1 'Answering' card

6 & 7 Adverse influences

2 & 3 Helpful influences

Yes or No —
A Simple Answering Spread

5.

The Suit of Cups

For the purposes of divination, the Suit of Cups represents:

1. The Emotional aspect of our Daily Lives
2. The Element of Water
3. The Three Watery Signs of the Zodiac — Pisces, Cancer and Scorpio
4. The letter Heh [emergence of energy into form] of the Tetragrammaton

Obviously, this means that if a majority of the Suit of Cups should appear in a Spread, then the Spread will relate to the Querent's emotional life and condition. It does *not* mean, however, that it will relate to the Querent's love life; and you must take care that you do not automatically assume this to be the case, as nothing could be further from the truth.

The word 'emotion' has no single well-defined meaning because it does not relate to a single well-defined state. Love is certainly an emotion; but it is not the only one. Rather it is the most attractive of which the human race is capable. Rage is an emotion. Terror, hatred and pity are all emotions too. The word 'love' itself demands qualification if it is to be correctly and accurately interpreted; and if you persist in equating the Suit of Cups with 'love', and interpreting the word 'love' to mean physical or romantic love, you are going to find yourself in the most horrendous difficulties.

One of the most important things to bear in mind when dealing with this Suit is that it is basically ambivalent in nature. It does not relate to *facts*, which are tangible and material, but to *feelings*, which are not. This problem is compounded by the fact that Tarot Cards very often reveal the surface of the Querent's mind *primarily*, and actuality only *obliquely*. For example, your Querent may *feel* that his immediate superior views him with considerable dislike, and is blocking his promotion for that reason. Because your Querent is firm in his belief that this is the case, the situation has become *real for him*, and your cards may very well, *on the surface*, appear to confirm his belief unconditionally. Further and more careful scrutiny of them, however, may reveal that your Querent's superior likes him well enough, but doubts his fitness for promotion, which is a very different kettle of fish, and creates a situation which your Querent must handle in a very different way. Again, your Querent may *feel* that a woman he is attracted to is attracted to him in return. If you read the Spread that reveals this situation in a facile way, you might confirm him in his belief, thus causing him to behave toward the woman in a specific way. This is all well and good if you have read the situation correctly. If you have not, your Querent will certainly suffer pain and embarrassment, and might become an object of ridicule.

Any Spread composed of a majority of the Suit of Cups must therefore be examined with the greatest care, and comment should only be forthcoming from you after prolonged scrutiny and thought. In fact it is often wisest when dealing with this Suit to look for a subsidiary majority (i.e., the next Suit numerically preponderating) to 'ground' your reading on some factual base before you utter a single word.

It is wise to remember too that when you are dealing with the emotions of others, you are walking on dangerous and shaky ground. The rule to follow here is very simple: the better you know your Querent personally, the more euphemistic you must be. One can be as blunt as one cares to be with strangers; they both expect and welcome it; friends prefer gentler treatment, and if your friendships are to survive your interest in the Tarot, you had better provide it!

There is a modifying principle built into the Tarot which you might find of assistance when you are rather more *au fait* with your Deck. For the present, it is best simply to learn it rather than attempt to use it, for it can be somewhat confusing to beginners.

Basically, the modifying principle works on the premise that every card in the Deck is strong or weak dependent upon the cards on either side of, above, or below it. Cards of friendly nature, or cards of the same Suit will prove a strengthening influence on any card, for better or worse according to Dignity. Cards of opposite nature, on the other hand, can greatly weaken or even negate altogether the card they surround, again for better or worse according to Dignity. Suits are considered to be *opposite* in nature as follows:

Wands are opposite to Cups, and vice versa.
Swords are opposite to Pentacles, and vice versa.

Hence, a Cup card surrounded by Wands will be weakened, or have little or no influence in the reading.

Suits are considered to be of friendly natures as follows:

Swords are friendly with Cups and Wands.
Wands are friendly with Swords and Pentacles.

This means that a Sword card surrounded with *either* Cups or Wands will be strengthened. If the Sword card is surrounded with Cups *and* Wands however, then the enmity of the two latter Suits must be taken into consideration *before* one considers their reaction on the central Sword card.

You can test the usefulness and validity of this modifying principle in practice at the end of this chapter if you wish — and without causing yourself too much confusion since you are only working with two Suits at present and the two Suits concerned are, of course, *opposite*, and therefore *mutually weakening* in nature. It would not be wise to make a habit of using this modifying principle, however, until you have had considerably more practice at just plain reading.

As was the case with the Suit of Wands, Significators may be chosen from the Suit of Cups without reference to Astrological data, and using only the physical colouring and age of your subject as guidelines. The physical characteristics appropriate to the Suit of Cups are as follows:

	Hair Colour	Eye Colour
Page	Brown	Blue or brown
Knight	Brown	Grey or blue
Queen	Golden brown	Blue
King	Fair	Blue

As usual, before you go on to the section dealing with the divinatory meanings of this Suit you should lay out the entire Suit in order on your silk scarf and pack all the cards you will not be using back into your wooden box. Cup cards are fairly easy to distinguish from any other Suit in most Decks, but check carefully to make sure you have the right cards in any case. As you work your way through the Suit, be sure to examine and 'mind's-eye-test' each card thoroughly as you deal with it, and don't forget to start your fantasy plays immediately you have written down the Ill-Dignified meaning of the Two of Cups.

When you have completed the last fantasy play using the Suit of Cups alone, search the portion of the Deck you have not been using, extract from it the 14 cards of the Suit of Wands, and pack the remaining two Suits and the Major Arcana back in your wooden box. Shuffle the Suits of Wands and Cups well together and *commence the fantasy play process all over again*, using both Suits and treating this set of fantasy plays exactly as if they were real readings. The best way to do this is to extract one of the 8 Court Cards available to you from the portion of the Deck you are using, shuffle the remaining cards and deal yourself six or seven of them off the top of the Deck in a line across the table. After you have 'read' these cards by making up a story from their given meanings, you should clear them away, deal yourself another set, and begin again. When you have done half a dozen or so of these 'readings' *you should go directly on to the Reader's Check List and the Instructions for the Spread*. Remember, the work you have done on this Chapter has 'primed' you mentally to perform the Practice Reading as well and as accurately as you possibly can at this time, so don't take a break before you start it.

The Ace of Cups

The Root of the Powers of Water

Numerical Value: 5
Season: Summer*
Direction: West*

Dignified: Love, joy, fertility and abundance. Faithfulness. Projects of a creative or artistic nature begun.

Ill-Dignified: Barrenness, either physical or of an emotional faculty. Emotional upsets. Loss of faith, unhappiness and dissatisfaction.

* Precise timing and distance according to Dignity as per previous note.

The Two of Cups

The Lord of Love

Numerical Value: 2

Dignified: The beginnings of a new romance, friendship or partnership. Harmony and co-operation. New ideas, generally generated by two people working together. Differences resolved.

Ill-Dignified: Quarrels and misunderstandings. Separation, divorce, love not returned or inequitable regard. Unfaithfulness.

The Three of Cups

The Lord of Abundance

Numerical Value: 3

Dignified: Fortunate conclusion of a valued project. A birth.* Renewed health and vitality. Great happiness and perhaps celebration.

Ill-Dignified: Excessive self-indulgence. Sensuality and selfishness. Exploitation of others. Obesity, promiscuity and over-indulgence.** Sometimes illnesses associated with smoking, drinking and over-eating.

*   A birth does not always signify a physical birth. The inception of a new business or project can equally be called 'a birth'.
** There is always a reason for self-destructive behaviour of this sort. You should therefore look for this root cause of the problem and *not* simply state the obvious. After all, if your Querent is over-eating he or she is well aware of it and does not need you to bring the subject up.

The Four of Cups

The Lord of Blended Pleasure

Numerical Value: 4

Dignified: Boredom and dissatisfaction. A time for re-evaluation of a too-familiar environment or lifestyle. A need to seek new goals, or a more stimulating way of life.

Ill-Dignified: Satiety and excess. A seeking after novelty and excitement for its own sake that brings little or fleeting pleasure. A low threshold of boredom.

The Five of Cups

The Lord of Loss in Pleasure

Numerical Value: 5

Dignified: Worry and regret, disappointment and loss. Dreams, legacies of an emotional or monetary nature. Broken engagements and emotional letdowns. A need to re-order to re-evaluate priorities.

Ill-Dignified: A way of life overturned. New alliances and expectations. Anxieties caused by unexpected and rapid change. Trouble from unexpected sources.

The Six of Cups

The Lord of Pleasure

Numerical Value: 6

Dignified: Pleasant memories, wishes fulfilled. Past work has brought present success. Past associations have brought present relationships. Harmony.

Ill-Dignified: Nostalgia. Vanity. Pride in past accomplishment proves a barrier to fresh achievement. A clinging to outworn customs or habits. Lack of concern for others.

The Seven of Cups

The Lord of Illusionary Success

Numerical Value: 7

Dignified:	Choice, sometimes between the mystical and the material. Too many opportunities may result in serious errors of judgement, if all are not carefully examined before the final choice is made.*
Ill-Dignified:	Self-delusion and fantasy. Lost opportunities. Reliance on false promises. A fear of success.

* This may of course refer to people, i.e., marriage and other partners.

The Eight of Cups

The Lord of Abandoned Success

Numerical Value: 8

Dignified: A turning point. A rejection of established modes of thought, social mores, relationships or lifestyle of something new and different.

Ill-Dignified: Restlessness and recklessness. A search for an ideal that leads to abandonment of a carefully built and well-founded way of life.

The Nine of Cups

The Lord of Material Happiness

Numerical Value: 9

Dignified: Contentment and physical well-being. Satisfaction. Material success and an assured future.

Ill-Dignified: Complacency. Vanity and self-indulgence. Spendthrift tendencies lead to shortage of money or loss of credit. Abuse of hospitality.

The Ten of Cups

The Lord of Perfected Success

Numerical Value: 10

Dignified: Happy family life. True friendship, lasting happiness and security.*

Ill-Dignified: Family quarrels. Loss of friendship. Sudden, violent disruption of an ordered environment, sometimes caused by children or young people. Look for signs of new births or adolescents.

* This card sometimes signifies a person who is 'in a rut'. They are quite happy, but it is a negative, rather than a positive state.

The Page of Cups

The Princess of the Waters;
The Lotus of the Palace of the Floods

Numerical Value: 7
Elemental Name: Earth of
                      Water

Dignified: A quiet, reflective and artistic person, gentle and kind, but dreamy at times. Dependent upon other cards: a messenger bringing news of a birth, engagement or marriage.

Ill-Dignified: A selfish and idle person, given to lies and harmful gossip. Dependent upon other cards: a deception will be uncovered.

The Knight of Cups

The Lord of the Waves and the Waters;
The King of the Hosts of the Sea

Numerical Value: 4
Elemental Name: Fire of
            Water

Dignified: An amiable and intelligent person, but a dreamer and easily led or discouraged. Dependent upon other cards: propositions, invitations, offers and opportunities.

Ill-Dignified: An idle person, and a congenital liar. Dependent upon other cards: trickery, embezzlement and fraud.

The Queen of Cups

Queen of the Thrones of the Waters

Numerical Value: 4
Elemental Name: Water of
Water

Dignified: An imaginative, affectionate and gifted woman, but lacking in common sense. Highly intuitive and sometimes psychic, but dreamy and easily influenced by other people, events, 'atmospheres'.

Ill-Dignified: An unreliable woman who cannot be trusted or depended upon, as her opinions change swiftly and without logical or just reason. A perverse woman, or one inclined to hysteria.

The King of Cups

Prince of the Chariot of the Waters

Numerical Value: 4
Elemental Name: Air of
Water

Dignified: A man of business or law. A skilled negotiator, kind, considerate and responsible, but ambitious. A man of ideas and agility of mind.

Ill-Dignified: A dishonest or unscrupulous man, likely to be double dealing. A violent and treacherous man.

Instructions for the Celtic Cross Spread

The Celtic Cross is a very useful general Spread, which can be used without any specific question ever being asked. If a majority should appear in this Spread, then the whole Spread should be read in the light of this majority. If no majority appears, then the Spread should be read generally, and in reference to the meaning assigned to each card placement by the Spread pattern, i.e., card number 9 'Hopes and Fears', and so on.

Cards should be read in numerical order, beginning with card number One, which overlays the Significator. The only difficulty you are likely to meet here is in reading card number 2, which has no obvious Dignity. Usually, this card is always read as being Dignified. I have found, however, that this does not always render a true account of the situation, and I personally therefore prefer to cast my eye over the Spread first and then actually *decide* upon a Dignity for it.

As you can see, there is some 'history' available in the Spread, as well as more than one hint of future developments. The Spread is said to have a three month validity as to both past and future. If you should find that the problem is of more than three months, standing, then take care not to promise your Querent a solution in three months. Sometimes, when a curiously long time lapse is covered by a Spread not designed to accommodate it, the problem is one that the Querent is unwilling to face or deal with, with the result that circumstances are not moving along as rapidly as they might, and you should not commit yourself as to timing in such a situation.

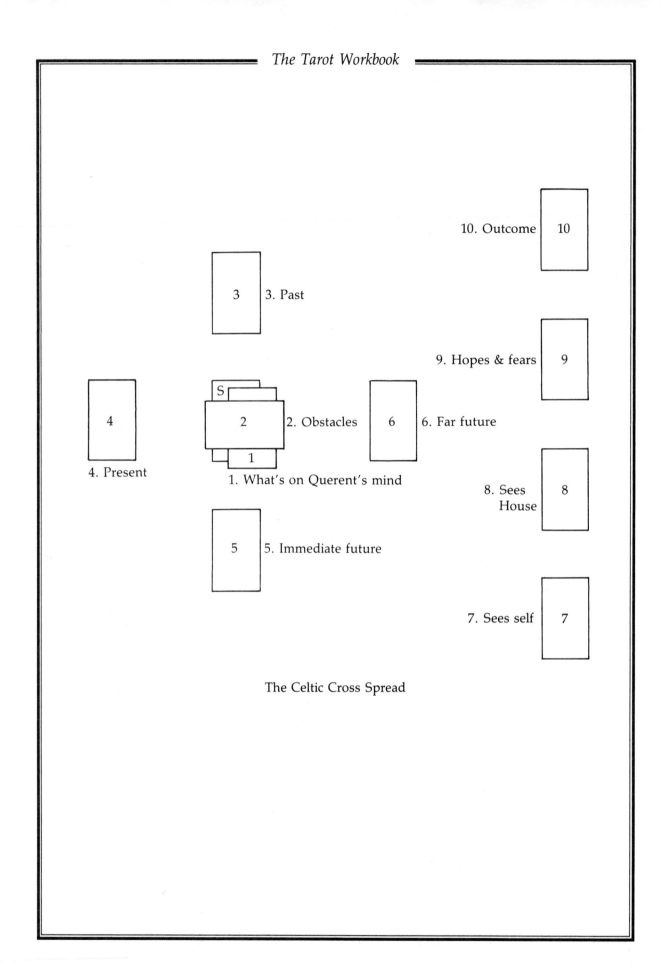

The Celtic Cross Spread

6.

The Suit of Swords

For the purposes of divination, the Suit of Swords represents:

1. The Mental aspect of our Daily Lives
2. The Element of Air
3. The Three Airy Signs of the Zodiac — Gemini, Libra and Aquarius
4. The letter Vau [stabilization of form] of the Tetragrammaton

Swords as a Suit have a bad reputation. They are said to portend argument and contention, illness and death, and to a certain degree this is true. These things are after all a part of life, and as a mirror of life, the Tarot must reflect them somewhere. You should bear in mind in this regard, however, that the Suit of Swords represents an intangible *mental activity* and is, like the Suit of Cups, ambivalent in nature. This means that the cards of this Suit also must be interpreted with extreme care.

Mental activity is a catch-all phrase. Hopes and fears, dreams and nightmares, fond imaginings and grim forebodings are all a form of mental activity, and all of them find expression in the Suit of Swords. None of them, however, need necessarily be in any way related to *real* situations, and so I would repeat: *Tarot cards very often reveal the surface of the Querent's mind primarily, and reality only obliquely.* Keep this phrase in the forefront of your mind when faced with a majority of this suit, and always look for a subsidiary majority with which to 'ground' your reading properly; you will find it an invaluable aid to proper perspective.

Sword majorities are extremely common and occur very much more often than one would expect. This is primarily due to the society we live in, which is, by and large, both dangerous and stressful. Road and industrial accidents, for instance, are at an unacceptably high level. Our environment is polluted on an unprecedented scale. Urban violence is on the rise and is terrifyingly random. The structure of the family is changing. Our increasingly technological and mechanized society can be frightening, alienating and frustrating as well as useful, and our future on a global level suddenly seems precarious and uncertain. We are being called upon, in short, to adapt with great rapidity to situations of increasing complexity which we are powerless to affect in any meaningful way. There are very few people today who are unaware of these facts, but while most of us deal with them moderately well, an increasing number of us do not, and nearly all of us think and worry about them periodically — particularly when our energies are at a low ebb or we are in a depressed state due to other and more immediate causes.

To all of the foregoing must be added the fact that death has replaced sex as the great unmentionable, and has, for very large numbers of people, ceased to be the natural thing that it is, and has become instead a faceless monster, Public Enemy Number One. This attitude too is the product of, and is daily reinforced by, the society we live in. Ours is a youth oriented society. We have more leisure, more money, more *toys* than we used to have. Circumstance has divorced us from the concept of death as a fact of life, and the vastly increased pleasure that we get out of life these days has caused a widespread *resentment* of the *idea* of death. We do not talk about it, and it is not, on the whole, very visible to us, being mostly confined to clinical environments rather than taking place in the home as it used to do. The orthodox churches, whose province it has traditionally been to guide us in our attitudes to death, have lost their hold on the public imagination. Consequently large numbers of people have little faith or belief in the idea of a life hereafter, and death has become possibly more mysterious and frightening than it has ever been at any other period of history. Death too, therefore, is something that we increasingly think and worry about.

Worries of this nature — death, unforeseen accident, serious illness, and just plain confusion in a sometimes incomprehensible world — are, along with more usual worries like money and marital upheavals, the stuff of which Sword majorities are made. Be aware that this is so, and handle these majorities for what they are — signs of stress and worry about situations that may well exist only in the mind of your Querent, the 'might be's' of his life. Check subsidiary majorities carefully, use your common sense, and bear in mind that *real* forecasts of death are very rare indeed, and form an unmistakable line-up within the Spread when they do appear. Until you are faced with such a situation — and believe me you will recognize it immediately when you *are* faced with it — do not let these Sword majorities bother you. They are inclined to appear to be forecasting disaster of holocaust dimension, but they are simply, alas, signs of the times.

This brings me to the vexed question of exactly what one should do on the rare occasion when one is faced with a real forecast of death, accident or serious illness. The answer is simple: nothing. Whether the threat be to the Querent direct or to his family or acquaintance, one can in fact do nothing, for nothing you can say, no foreknowledge that you can impart, can alter in any way the mainstream pattern — the Karma if you like — of your Querent's life, or the lives of his family or friends. You cannot warn. You cannot (obviously) make a bald statement of impending doom. You cannot, in the last analysis, even *hint*, for you will only disturb and upset your Querent to no useful purpose.

This is naturally a very disturbing situation for any reader, and it can be a galling one for the reader who is personally aquainted with his Querent, or simply takes pride in accuracy. I would ask you to remember, however, that neither personal friendship nor the very natural and human desire to be *right* can ever take precedence over your responsibility to your Querent. This responsibility can be simply stated, for it exists within clearly defined limits. It is your job, as a reader, to state the problem, expose its roots (thus clarifying the situation) and thereafter advise your Querent in such a way that he or she leaves your presence in a more positive and cheerful frame of mind. Since foreknowledge of some impending disaster about which he can do absolutely nothing is unlikely to send your Querent away jolly and relaxed, it is obviously not permissible to impart information of that nature.

Most importantly of course, you should bear in mind that it is not impossible — indeed it is exceedingly common — for even the most accomplished of us to be absolutely categorically *wrong* about a reading. This, if nothing else, should cause you to pause and *think* before you overstep the line of what is right and cause another person to endure unnecessary agony of mind.

As usual, before you go on to the section dealing with the divinatory meanings of this Suit you should lay out the entire Suit on your silk scarf, checking carefully to ensure that you are working with the right cards. As you work your way through the Suit do not neglect to examine and 'mind's-eye-test' each card thoroughly and remember that you should begin your fantasy plays directly you have written down the Ill-Dignified meaning of the Two of Swords.

This time, when you have completed the last fantasy play using the Suit of Swords alone, you should search the Deck and extract the Suits of Wands and Cups, shuffle the three Suits that you have learned to date together and commence the fantasy play reading process exactly as you did in the last session. After you have completed half a dozen or so of these 'readings' go on *without pause* to the Reader's Check List and the Practice Reading.

It would be a good idea at this point to use an absent friend as your subject for the practice reading — and preferably a friend whose Astrological sign you are *genuinely* unaware of. This will help you to get used to choosing a Significator from a physical description only, and also to reading without the 'feedback' that is usually generated by the presence of the Querent. It will also enable you, if you write out your findings, to check your accuracy with your friend at a later date. A general question as to your friend's mental or emotional state is the best sort of problem to set yourself, and if you formulate the question clearly in your mind before you begin, and *visualize* your friend (this is best achieved by 'mind's-eye-examining' your friend just as you 'mind's-eye-examine' your cards) while you are shuffling the cards, you should get very acceptable results. If you cannot find your chosen subject's physical characteristics in the preceding chapters or in this one, please turn to page 87 and look for them there.

The physical characteristics that are associated with the Suit of Swords are as follows:

	Hair Colour	Eye Colour
Page	Light brown	Blue
Knight	Dark	Dark
Queen	Light brown	Grey
King	Dark brown	Dark

The Ace of Swords

The Root of the Powers of Air

Numerical Value: 5
Season: Autumn
Direction: East

Dignified: A new beginning, a rebirth. Victory, success, triumph, great force. A complete change of mind, including all aspects of the Querent's life.

Ill-Dignified: Destruction, violence, misuse of power. Death sometimes, depending upon other cards.

The Two of Swords

The Lord of Peace Restored

Numerical Value: 2

Dignified: Relief. Differences resolved. Truce, peace restored, pleasure after pain. A weight lifted from the mind.

Ill-Dignified: Release. Movement of affairs away from difficulty, but sometimes in the wrong direction and upon misguided or willfully misleading advice.

The Three of Swords

The Lord of Sorrow

Numerical Value: 3

Dignified: Strife, conflict, heartbreak, tears and separations.* Quarrels and disruption.

Ill-Dignified: Discord, confusion, loss, treachery and sorrow.

* Separations in this context means those separations not ratified in the eyes of the law, i.e., marriage partners living apart but having no legal Separation Agreement, or partners in a business that is inactive but not legally dissolved.

The Four of Swords

The Lord of Rest from Strife

Numerical Value: 4

Dignified: Hospitalization, rest, convalescence, recovery. A sabbatical, a retreat, solitude. Relief from sorrow or anxiety.

Ill-Dignified: Enforced seclusion. Imprisonment. Banishment from social affairs in which the Querent was used to take part.

The Five of Swords

The Lord of Defeat

Numerical Value: 5

Dignified: Failure, trouble, defeat, loss, cowardice. Negative thinking or negative attitudes.

Ill-Dignified: Weakness, indecision and sometimes paranoia.

The Six of Swords

The Lord of Earned Success

Numerical Value: 6

Dignified: Long journeys. Passage away from pain or difficulty. Obstacles overcome. Success after trouble and anxiety.

Ill-Dignified: Retreat from difficulties that brings temporary relief. One obstacle has barely been overcome before another takes its place. Struggle.

The Seven of Swords

The Lord of Unstable Effort

Numerical Value: 7

Dignified: Short journeys, change of job or residence — often both. Restlessness and instability of purpose ensures that no real progress is made.

Ill-Dignified: Indecision, laziness and failure of nerve. Reluctance to complete what has been well begun.

The Eight of Swords

The Lord of Shortened Force

Numerical Value: 8

Dignified:	Restriction, crisis, enforced isolation, censure and jealousy — often from family or workmates.
Ill-Dignified:	Freedom, release and relaxation, obtained by distancing the problem rather than solving it. Hard and uncongenial work for little reward.

The Nine of Swords

The Lord of Despair and Cruelty

Numerical Value: 9

Dignified: Bad dreams or premonitions. Deception, depression and suffering. Violence, scandal and loss. Perhaps the death of a loved one pressaged.

Ill-Dignified: Malice. Misery and despair. Isolation, imprisonment, suicide and institutionalization generally.

The Ten of Swords

The Lord of Ruin

Numerical Value: 10

Dignified: Sudden misfortune. Accident. Muggings or personal robbery. Desolation, disruption and ruin.

Ill-Dignified: Violent and extreme change. Death sometimes.

The Page of Swords

The Princess of the Rushing Winds; The Lotus of the Palace of Air

Numerical Value: 7
Elemental Name: Earth of
Air

Dignified: A person of grace, dexterity and vigilance. Very acute and subtle, a negotiator. Depending on other cards — a message pressaging change.

Ill-Dignified: A devious, frivolous and cunning person, possibly vindictive and two-faced. Depending on other cards: ill health or unforeseen events causing changes of plan.

The Knight of Swords

Lord of the Winds and the Breezes; King of the Spirits of Air

Numerical Value: 4
Elemental Name: Fire of
Air

Dignified: An active, clever individual, subtle and skilful, but inclined to be domineering. Depending on other cards: events moving swiftly into or out of the Querent's life, for good or ill.

Ill-Dignified: A deceitful and sly individual, secretive and belligerent. Depending upon other cards: quarrels.

The Queen of Swords

The Queen of the Thrones of Air

Numerical Value: 4
Elemental Name: Water
of Air

Dignified: An intelligent and complex woman, highly perceptive and quick-witted. Often skilful at balancing opposing factions one against the other to further her ends.

Ill-Dignified: An unreliable woman, deceitful and sly. A narrow minded and intolerant woman. A gossip.

The King of Swords

The Prince of the Chariots of the Winds

Numerical Value: 4
Elemental Name: Air of
                Air

Dignified:	A rational man with a logical and inventive turn of mind, but sometimes overcautious and old fashioned. A man of law and an upholder of authority.
Ill-Dignified:	An obstinate man of calculating and impersonal temperament. Sometimes malicious, unjust and cruel.

Instructions for the Qabalistic Cross Spread

This Spread is designed to give an overall picture of any given situation, including past, present and future circumstances, together with the feelings and attitudes of people other than the Querent who might be involved in the situation.

This is not an 'answering' Spread, and so you should ensure that your Querent phrases his question in a generalized way that does not require an absolute answer. Questions beginning 'When will I...' or 'Will I...' are therefore unacceptable for the purposes of this particular Spread, while questions such as 'What are the circumstances behind...' do very well.

Once again, the Significator is overlaid by another card, this time card number Four, which is usually taken to signify the Querent's state of mind. This card should be read, as was the case with the previous Spread, *before* all the other cards.

Cards numbered Thirteen, Twelve and Eleven should next be read, *beginning with card number Thirteen*. This Spread is usually understood to take into account circumstances three months into the past, and three months into the future. Card number Thirteen is therefore considered to be *furthest away in time* insofar as the *past* is concerned, for as you can see, cards Thirteen, Twelve and Eleven represent the *past*.

Cards numbered One, Two and Three should be read next, commencing with card number One. These three cards represent *present circumstances*.

Cards numbered Ten, Nine and Eight should be read next *and in that order*, for these three cards represent *future circumstances*, and card number Eight is held in this instance to be *furthest away in time*.

The whole reading should then be read again in the light of cards numbered Five, Six and Seven, which represent *the feelings of the other people involved in the situation*. Interestingly, this aspect of the reading often contrasts or openly conflicts with the evidence of card number Four, which represents the mental condition of the Querent. This process of reading the circumstances upon their own merits, and then in the light of the feelings of others, and then contrasting the whole with the attitude of the Querent, produces a very good overall picture of a situation, and it is surprising how the 'feeling' of the reading changes as one approaches it from a series of different angles in this way.

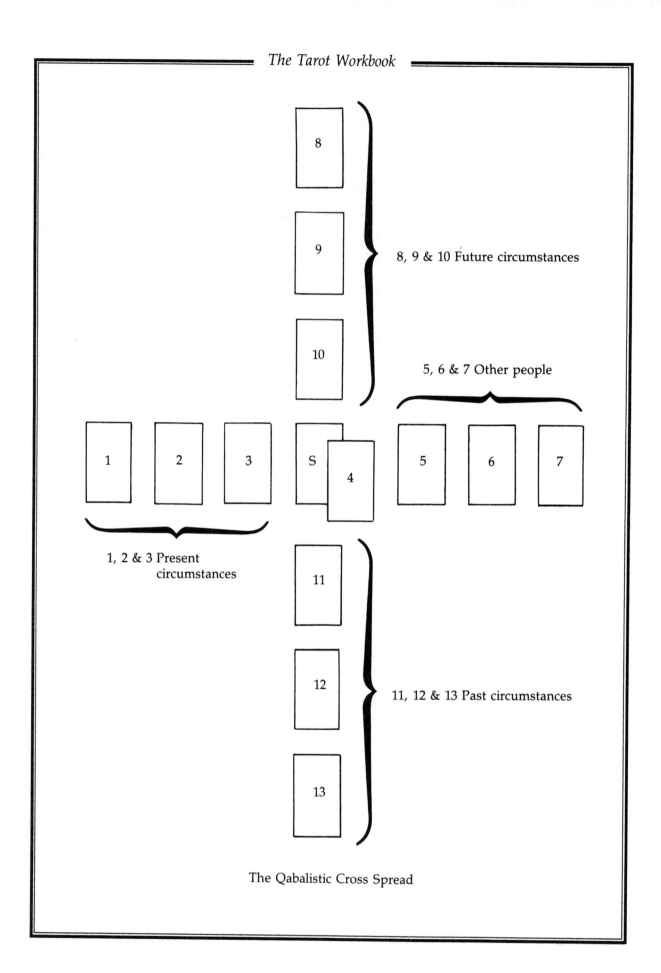

8, 9 & 10 Future circumstances

5, 6 & 7 Other people

1, 2 & 3 Present circumstances

11, 12 & 13 Past circumstances

The Qabalistic Cross Spread

7.

The Suit of Pentacles

For the purposes of divination, the Suit of Pentacles represents:

1. The Material aspect of our Daily Lives
2. The Element of Earth
3. The Three Earthy Signs of the Zodiac — Taurus, Capricorn and Virgo
4. The letter Heh (final) [completion of energy into form] of the Tetragrammaton

The Suit of Pentacles is the Suit of money and material things, and is perhaps the most straightforward of all the Suits to deal with. In many ways it is also the most useful, for it is wholly concerned with the tangible; the here and now; the absolutely real. There are no ifs, ands or buts about this suit, and because of its down-to-earth nature, it makes an excellent subsidiary majority.

A *majority* of this suit, on the other hand, can be extremely difficult to deal with. There is no ambivalence about it, of course; quite the opposite. The difficulty here lies in avoiding *the mere recitation of fact*. It may be interesting to your Querent that you are able to reel off the facts of his life with a large degree of accuracy, but it is not at all helpful to him, and so — paradoxically — this most 'real' of all Suits *must* be read only in the light of its subsidiary back-up.

Basically, majorities and subsidiaries serve to give subject and accent to a reading. If, for example, a majority of Wands appears with an underlying subsidiary of Pentacles, then the subject of the reading will be a business or career opportunity or project, and it will be the *project itself* that is of primary importance, and *not* the fiscal factors underlying it — despite the fact that these might cause the project to founder on the shores of insufficient cash-flow! If the situation is reversed, however, and there appears a majority of Pentacles with an underlying subsidiary of Wands, it will be the *fiscal factor* that is of primary importance, and the project will be secondary to it.

This is best illustrated by taking as an example an imaginary Querent who is seeking and has the opportunity of taking up new employment. In this instance, should a majority of *Wands* appear with underlying subsidiary of Pentacles, *job satisfaction* would most probably be the primary object of the Querent's search for employment; salary and benefits taking second place. If on the other hand the situation were reversed, causing Pentacles to replace Wands as the majority, then the primary object of the Querent's search for employment would be *fiscal*, and job satisfaction would take second place.

Eventually, you will be able to lay out a Spread, spot its main theme, and tie up its subsidiaries instantly. This is a knack, like riding a bicycle, that comes suddenly, and is just as suddenly effortless. It cannot, unfortunatley be *taught* by one individual to another; but can only be acquired by those who strive to possess it.

Before you go on to the section dealing with the divinatory meanings of this suit, lay the cards of the Suit out as usual on your silk scarf. There should be no need at this point to check that you are using the correct cards because you should by now be quite intimately acquainted with the greater portion of your Deck, but check in any case. It is better to be absolutely sure that you are doing the right thing. As you work your way through the Suit examine the cards carefully and perform the mind's-eye-test on each one of them, not forgetting to commence with your fantasy plays immediately you have written down the Ill-Dignified meaning of the Two of Pentacles. When you have completed the last fantasy play using the Suit of Pentacles alone, extract the other three Suits from the remainder of your Deck, and using the entire Minor Arcana complete *at least* half a dozen fantasy play readings. The more of these readings you complete at this time the better off you will be. Using the complete Minor Arcana is somewhat different, and rather more complex, than using the odd portion of it, and you must work to accustom yourself to the new dimensions — mental and physical — of your Deck.

From now on, some part of your daily revision should be given over to creative use of your cards, and if you use them as you should, and consistently practise your fantasy play readings, you may find that you become subject to a new — and very common — phenomenon. You may find that it is suddenly very hard to focus mentally with any clarity on your cards; that it is hard to concentrate; that the given meanings have become blurred or vague in your mind, and that your mind is wandering into channels that have (apparently) very little to do with the card or cards that you have been working with. You may find yourself, in short, in a 'daydream state'. This is perfectly natural, and should on no account be discouraged. You should not try to 'snap out of it', or become alarmed or irritated or discouraged. Eventually, this will stop happening; for the moment it is simply a sign that you are beginning to learn to understand the language of the Tarot as it *should* be understood, and you should simply note, if you can, where these little mental digressions lead you, and when they are over, try *consciously* to trace the origins of your train of thought in the pictures on the cards you have been using.

The Practice Reading for this session is the most complex you have faced so far. It is extra-important this time, therefore, to go on with it *immediately* you have completed your fantasy play readings. You may want, or find it easier, to read, once again, for an absent Querent, and this is quite acceptable. The physical characteristics applicable to the Suit of Pentacles are as follows:

	Hair Colour	Eye Colour
Page	Rich brown	Dark
Knight	Dark brown	Dark
Queen	Dark	Dark
King	Dark	Dark

The Ace of Pentacles

The Root of the Powers of Earth

Numerical Value: 5
Season: Winter
Direction: North

Dignified: A change for the better financially. The beginnings of a period of financial gain, and material comfort.

Ill-Dignified: Greed, miserliness, lack of faith in anything beyond this world, and dependence upon physical pleasures for all happiness.

The Two of Pentacles

The Lord of Harmonious Change

Numerical Value: 2

Dignified:
Constant fluctuation and change in fortunes make new projects difficult to launch. Established business needs careful handling. A need to budget carefully. A warning to avoid purchasing on credit.

Ill-Dignified:
Reckless spending. Fecklessness. Insufficient effort. Inability to complete a project — or keep a job — due to concentration on the pleasures of the moment. Debt.

The Three of Pentacles

The Lord of Material Works

Numerical Value: 3

Dignified: Business opportunities. Success through effort and hard work. Increase of material things and gain in commerce.

Ill-Dignified: Preoccupation with gain. Hoarding and miserliness. Opportunities passed up due to fear of loss.

The Four of Pentacles

The Lord of Earthly Power

Numerical Value: 4

Dignified:	Material stability. Promotion. Increase of power through wealth and influence. Establishment of a project on a successful footing.
Ill-Dignified:	Greed, suspicion and lack of enterprise due to fear of loss. An inability to delegate authority.

The Five of Pentacles

The Lord of Material Trouble

Numerical Value: 5

Dignified:	Loss of money or position. Financial difficulty. Poverty and struggle. Redundancy.
Ill-Dignified:	Unemployment long continued. Hardship and financial distress.

The Six of Pentacles

The Lord of Material Success

Numerical Value: 6

Dignified: Philanthopy. Patronage. Charity, gifts and awards. Solvency in material affairs.

Ill-Dignified: Loss through theft or carelessness. Prodigality.

The Seven of Pentacles

The Lord of Success Unfulfilled

Numerical Value: 7

Dignified: The failure of a promising project. Unprofitable speculation. Charitable work undertaken for no reward. Profitable employment neglected through lack of interest.

Ill-Dignified: Financial problems, bankruptcy and loss. Gambling sometimes.

The Eight of Pentacles

The Lord of Prudence

Numerical Value: 8

Dignified: Prudence. Industriousness. Skill in material affairs or handiwork. Gain of money in small sums. Carefulness in respect of money. Savings. Conservative investments, stocks and bonds. Diplomacy.

Ill-Dignified: Sharp or dishonest dealings. Misuse of skill to improper ends.

The Nine of Pentacles

The Lord of Material Gain

Numerical Value: 9

Dignified: Money from unexpected sources. Inheritances. Winnings. Settlements and monetary gifts. Unearned income.*

Ill-Dignified: Tainted or stolen money. Theft or embezzlement.

                * Unearned income can mean alimony, dividends, etc.

The Ten of Pentacles

The Lord of Wealth

Numerical Value: 10

Dignified: Prosperity. Property. Inherited wealth. Material security founded upon the work of others.

Ill-Dignified: The restrictive effects of great wealth. Problems with wills or trusts. Disagreement about money within the family. Litigation.

The Page of Pentacles

The Princess of the Echoing Hills; The Rose of the Palace of Earth

Numerical Value: 7
Elemental Name: Earth of
                   Earth

Dignified: A thrifty and conscientious person. A persevering scholar. Gracious, careful and kind.

Ill-Dignified: A wasteful and prodigal person, over-meticulous in small things. Depending upon other cards: unfavourable news regarding financial matters.

The Knight of Pentacles

The Lord of the Wild and Fertile Land;
The King of the Spirits of Earth

Numerical Value: 4
Elemental Name: Fire of
                   Earth

Dignified: A practical person of conventional virtues or views. Patient, hardworking, and clever with material things, but rather slow, and inclined to lack awareness of the feelings of others.

Ill-Dignified: An avaricious and grasping person, complacent and rather timid. Depending upon other cards: monetary affairs at a standstill or breakeven.

The Queen of Pentacles

The Queen of the Thrones of Earth

Numerical Value: 4
Elemental Name: Water
of Earth

Dignified: A shrewd, sensible and down-to-earth woman, but loving splendour and personal display.

Ill-Dignified: A changeable woman, narrow in outlook and suspicious of what she does not understand. Grasping and careful and yet a spendthrift in matters that concern herself.

The King of Pentacles

The Prince of the Chariot of Earth

Numerical Value: 4
Elemental Name: Air of
                 Earth

Dignified:

A steady, methodical and reliable man, loyal, trustworthy and patient, but slow to think and act. Depending upon other cards: increase of wealth, establishment in a profession or large corporate entities.

Ill-Dignified:

A dull and materialistic person. An obstinate, heavy-handed and sometimes tyrannical person.

Instructions for the Planetary Deal Answering Spread

Despite the fact that the Planetary Deal Spread is primarily an answering Spread, it gives a very good overall picture of the Querent's situation. Card number 2, which holds the 'solution' or 'answer' for the purposes of this Spread, is really only providing the answer to a situation revealed by a *majority*, and every card in this Spread can and should be read on its own merits and relating to the meaning assigned to it *by its position in the Spread*, as well as with reference to the problem revealed by the majority.

For example, assuming that a majority of Wands appears, each card should be read:

a) in the light of the majority; and
b) card by card, i.e. card number One would be read upon its own merits, as a card revealing 'matters of the home'. Card number Two would be read upon its own merits, as a card revealing 'matters of business', and so on.

The reading from the viewpoint of the majority, however, should *always* be dealt with first.

Cards of this Spread can and ought to be paired and read in juxtaposition, i.e., the card in the position of the Moon should be paired with that in the position of the Sun; the card in the position of Venus with that in the position of Mars, and so on. When reading by this method, or for the purposes of a majority, the solution or answer to the reading will be found in the card representing Mercury, the reconciler.

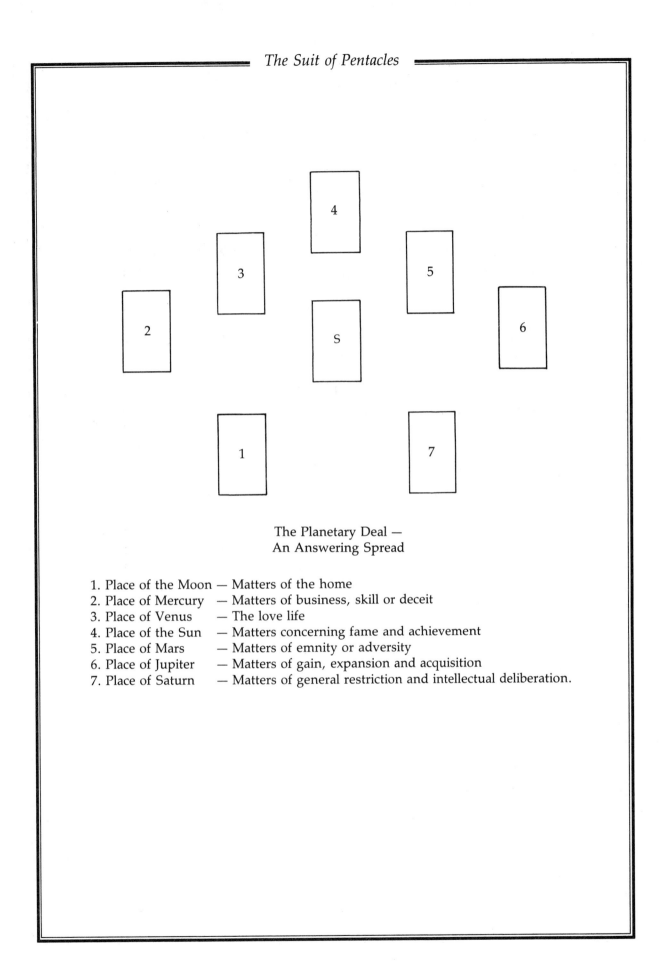

The Planetary Deal —
An Answering Spread

1. Place of the Moon — Matters of the home
2. Place of Mercury — Matters of business, skill or deceit
3. Place of Venus — The love life
4. Place of the Sun — Matters concerning fame and achievement
5. Place of Mars — Matters of emnity or adversity
6. Place of Jupiter — Matters of gain, expansion and acquisition
7. Place of Saturn — Matters of general restriction and intellectual deliberation.

8.

An Introduction to the Major Arcana

The Major Arcana constitutes the most important, meaningful and revealing part of the Tarot Deck, and consists of twenty-two picture cards with a descriptive name or title at the foot of each card.

The cards of the Major Arcana are not divided into Suits like the cards of the Minor Arcana, nor is there any card of the Major Arcana that can really be considered suitable for use as a Significator, although some systems do advocate this usage. This is because the cards of the Major Arcana do not represent people, situations or events like the cards of the Minor Arcana, but *Archetypal Forces, Powers* and *Elements in Nature* instead. These forces, powers and elements in nature appear on the face of each card symbolized by a scene, design or mandala, or personified by a figure or figures.

For the purposes of divination, Major Arcana cards are usually understood to represent the *Psychological State* of the Querent, or his *Reaction* to the people, situations and events of his life.

Like the Minor Arcana, the Major Arcana has basic elemental and astrological attributions. The attributions of the Major Arcana, however, refer not to groups of cards as was the case with the Minor Arcana, but to *each individual card*. In this way, *twelve* Major Arcana cards are attibuted to signs of the Zodiac, *seven* are attributed to Planets, and *three* are attributed to Elements.

These attributions, which are set forth more fully in the sections dealing with the divinatory meanings of the Major Arcana, form the basis for the simple numerical value that you will recall is used for counting the cards in complicated Spreads. Thus:

Any card that is attributed to a Sign of the Zodiac has a simple numerical value of Twelve.

Any card that is attributed to a Planet has a simple numerical value of *nine* as per the ancient astrological system; i.e., seven planets plus the two nodal points of the Moon.

Any card that is attributed to an Element has a simple numerical value of Three.

The number of Elements is reduced to three when dealing with the Major Arcana because this Arcana is not considered to relate to the mundane physical world, and the Element of Earth is therefore omitted from the count, although it can in fact be attributed to the card entitled 'The Universe', along with the Planet Saturn.

It is very important when dealing with the Major Arcana to remember that these simple numerical values are *for counting purposes only*. You must not confuse them with the other numbers also associated with the Major Arcana. For instance, there is also attributed to each Major Arcana card:

1. A Key Number
2. A Face Number
3. One of the Twenty-Two Letters of the Hebrew Alphabet.

Key Numbers run eleven through thirty-two, and serve to show the position of each Major Arcana card upon the glyph or mandala known as the Tree of Life. These numbers will be dealt with at length in a later chapter, but will appear in the relevant place in the section dealing with divinatory meanings of the Major Arcana so that you may become used to them, and able to follow the information that will be given you later more easily. Key Numbers do *not* appear anywhere on the face of the actual card.

Face Numbers appear in roman numerals at the top of each card and run from zero through twenty-one. Face numbers show the order in which the Major Arcana cards appear within the Tarot Deck.

Hebrew Letters were attributed to the cards comparatively recently, and serve to further relate the Deck to the Tree of Life and the Hebrew system of philosophy known as the Qabalah, which forms the basis of the Western Esoteric Tradition. Hebrew letters too will be dealt with in a later chapter, but like the Key Numbers (and all the other basic attributions discussed in this Chapter) they should be learned *now*, since they are of great importance, and you should at least be able to recognize and transliterate them as they appear. Hebrew letters therefore also appear in the relevant places in the sections dealing with divinatory meanings of the Major Arcana, together with the English translation of each letter.

Although it is not possible to identify with any exactitude the precise source of the Tarot Deck or of the images and designs that appear in it, it seems almost certain that the figures, scenes and symbols on these cards are drawn primarily from classical myth (although some of them display Biblical imagery and yet others bear medieval alchemical symbolism). This latter is a very specialized subject that has no place in a book of this kind, but a short Mythological Note appears at the foot of each of the ordinary divinatory meanings of these cards. These notes, however, are just that: notes. They are not detailed analyses of the cards, or of the myths that have been associated with the cards by various scholars over the years. Because myth has had an enormous influence on the design of the Major Arcana, I would strongly recommend that you do *not* simply read these notes and pass on to other things. It would be a much better idea to either buy or borrow one of the better books on mythology (a Bullfinch, for example, or a Larousse) and read the stories concerned as you go along. There is no need to spend 'classroom-time' doing this, but you should find *some* time for it. It is very important and will assist you enormously in coming to an understanding of the meanings that have been allotted to these cards and which otherwise might appear arbitrary or even nonsensical.

Because the Major Arcana has no natural division, the section dealing with divinatory meanings of the Major Arcana has been artificially divided into sections, each of which contains five or six cards. These divisions *are* arbitrary; there is no reason for their existence save our convenience.

At first glance, five or six cards per chapter might seem very little to be getting on with after the fourteen cards per chapter of the preceding section of the book. You will find, however, that if you are following the instructions carefully, and working properly, you may be progressing more slowly than ever before. You should not be discouraged if this turns out to be the case. Major Arcana cards are a very different kettle of fish to Minor Arcana cards, and the by-rote information that goes with them is more difficult to absorb and therefore more time consuming.

You should progress through the sections dealing with the divinatory meanings of the Major Arcana in exactly the same way, and using exactly the same methods, as were used to deal with the divinatory meanings of the Minor Arcana, taking particular care not to neglect your 'fantasy plays', or your 'mind's eye examination' of each card, which are doubly important processes now.

As usual, there is a Spread on which to practise at the end of each section. You will see that these Spreads are becoming progressively more complex and difficult. If you feel at any time that you simply cannot handle the fresh information input *and* a fresh Spread, then use the Spreads you are more familiar with, but on no account should you neglect to do a Spread at all.

Make sure before you commence the chapters dealing with divinatory meanings of the Major Arcana that you have understood and assimilated the contents of this chapter, *and all of the foregoing chapters.* Try to pinpoint any 'blind' spots you may have developed for the basic attributions by writing them out, and then work quickly through the four Suits of the Minor Arcana, calling out the two divinatory meanings of each card as you go along. If you find there is anything you have forgotten, or some meaning that persistently slips your memory, write it down several times immediately and then re-check yourself on those points later. Don't neglect to check yourself on the relationships between the Suits, the physical descriptions that can be used to find a Significator in lieu of more exact information, and the seasons and directions that relate to each Ace. Make sure that you can draw each one of the Spreads you have used so far accurately from memory.

Remember, there is no point in going on now if you are not absolutely up to date with your work so far.

9.

Signs and Symbols

By now, and always supposing that you have done the work demanded of you thus far properly, you will have come to the realization that if you perform certain actions with a pack of Tarot cards, you will obtain results that are in many ways difficult to reconcile with the actions you have performed; i.e., you will have recognized that you are able to shuffle together fifty-six pieces of ordinary pasteboard and come up with a fairly accurate prognostication of future events.

In the course of the next four chapters, we will examine some of the reasons you are achieving this result; and we will commence the process by examining how Tarot cards are constructed.

Despite its obvious similarity to an ordinary pack of playing cards, the Tarot is really less a deck of cards than a picture book. It is, of course, rather different from the average book, since it has no cover, no binding, no fixed unchallenged order of pages and no known author; but it is nevertheless still a **book**, with **text** (translations from which you have learned as Divinatory Meanings) and a **pictorial alphabet**.

Pictorial languages like the one in which the book of the Tarot is written are a very ancient concept indeed, but because of their special qualities they are an ongoing part of the human experience, and you are much more familiar with their sign/symbol alphabets than you might imagine. The designs shown below, for example, are modern symbols taken from a contemporary pictorial language:

Like all symbols, the ones shown here are *things* that stand for other *things* — or more precisely they are things that stand for other concepts.

Usually, the concepts that are chosen to be portrayed symbolically are the abstract ones; like honour for example, or patience. Symbols give expression to the invisible, intangible qualities of these concepts by embodying them in visible, tangible objects. Thus, the owl is the symbol of wisdom, the lion is the symbol of courage, and so on.

The second set of designs shown here are contemporary *signs*. Signs are pictures and designs that are used to convey information and represent ideas. The distinction between signs and symbols is a narrow but important one: signs are often self-explanatory; but symbols must generally be learned. Take, for example, the modern sign/symbol illustrated below:

This sign/symbol means 'First Aid Station'. The sign portion of this design consists of a human hand, the index finger of which is encased in bandage, so most people would find it possible to associate this portion of the picture with the concepts minor ailment or minor injury without too much difficulty; simply because they have seen and experienced the situation shown in the picture countless times.

The symbol portion of the design, however, might present somewhat of a problem — unless the onlooker is familiar with the symbol and has learned its meaning. ✚ of course symbolizes two concepts in this context. The first is Red Cross, an international Christian medical organization. The second is Hospital. Thus the *sign* portion of the design *modifies* the *symbol* portion, so that the basic meaning of the whole becomes 'Simple Medical Care Available Here.'

Signs are usually more readily comprehensible than symbols because signs are more often than not *pictographs*, while symbols are *ideographs*.

Pictographs are pictures that use mundane objects or situation scenes in order to tell stories. The pictograph/sign illustrated below, for example, was purpose designed for use at the Tokyo Olympic Games in 1964. It is a picture of a very mundane object — a cup and saucer — and is one of the huge crop of signs and symbols that has grown up to help us meet the special demands of our society — a world oriented society with a high incidence of international trade and travel. It is a good example of an efficient and well designed pictograph:

Unfortunately, of course, not all pictographs are as purpose perfect as this one. Lack of an absolutely precise meaning and the consequent possibility of misinterpretation are a major failing of pictographs, and this is not always the result of poor design, as this next illustration shows:

Icy road? Winding road? The artist has done his best, but the result is still somewhat ambiguous. The real meaning is: Slippery When Wet.

The next illustration is a *symbol* and an *ideograph*. It too is a purpose-made design, but — as you can see — it is abstract, and very difficult to interpret on a stand-alone basis. Indeed, unless you are familiar with this symbol, or have seen it frequently in its proper context, you are unlikely to be able to work out its meaning, or even imagine where it might belong:

TTTTTTT
TTTTTTT
TTTTTTT

It is in fact the standardized international map symbol for corn, and it illustrates very well the major failing of ideographs. It is worthwhile noting, however, that although this symbol must be learned before it can be used and understood, once it has been learned it completely lacks the ambiguity inherent in sign/pictographs like:

SCHOOL CROSSING

Sometimes, the signs and symbols of a pictorial communication system are qualified, clarified and restricted by the addition of less universal but more precise letter alphabet signs and symbols. The meaning of this modern highway symbol, for example, has been reinforced by the addition of the word: 'Stop'.

The individual letters of the word 'Stop' are symbols, but they are not pictographs or ideographs — although they may originally have stemmed from either or both. The letters of the English alphabet as they stand today are *pure symbols*, representing the sounds we make when we speak. The spoken words themselves, of course, are pure symbols too — symbols for the concepts, ideas and realities they convey to the listener.

The value of pure symbols lies in their precision, and their capability of defining concepts and ideas within narrow parameters. Consider, for example, the subtly differing shades of meaning conveyed by the words: fat, plump and obese. All describe a single condition, but each conveys a well-defined and quite precise state within that condition. Neither pictographs nor ideographs are capable of quite this sort of precision, but both can be said to lack the major drawback of language symbols — parochialism.

All pure symbols are parochial in nature. To understand the word 'stop', for example, it is necessary not only to be able to speak and understand the language that the letter symbols represent, but to be able to *read* the symbols as well. Thus ready comprehension of the written word 'Stop' is automatically limited to English speaking people who have successfully learned to read. It is this parochialism that makes letter alphabet systems — and all pure symbol systems — very poor 'reinforcement tools' for pictorial language systems. The sign illustrated below, for example, illustrates the parochialism of language symbols perfectly. It is the Chinese version of the road sign meaning:

No Parking!

From the modern examples shown above, it is easy to see why signs and symbols have always been, and still are, used so extensively in everyday life. We — and countless millions of people like us all over the world — see, 'read', understand and respond to thousands of signs and symbols like them every day. They direct, warn and advise us — almost wordlessly — in the only universal language we as yet possess, and life without them would be inexpressibly more difficult and confusing. Some of them — like the ones that help us use our roads and highways safely and correctly — we learn deliberately; but by far the greater number are simply assimilated into our sign/symbol vocabulary as we go through life, without much conscious effort on our part. All, however, are necessary to the efficient functioning of the modern world, and — more importantly — all fulfil the requirements of good signs/symbols: *They transcend cultural and linguistic barriers, and convey information rapidly and concisely.*

This latter point is vital to a realistic understanding of the Tarot, for it goes some way toward explaining one of the reasons (but not the only one) that the Tarot, which has survived for many centuries comparatively unchanged, was originally designed and constructed as it is — from pictures.

Consider, for example, the two cards illustrated below:

 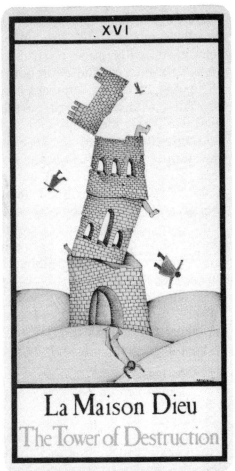

Card A   Card B

As you can see, they are essentially the same — or rather the all important picture portion of each card is to all intents and purposes the same. The language symbols, however — despite the fact that the language symbols used on both cards are drawn from the same symbol system — are *not* the same, and if you do not speak French, the legend at the foot of card B will mean nothing to you.

The sign/symbol system of which the Tarot is constructed is not, of course, a contemporary one, but some of its signs and symbols will nevertheless be familiar to you because they have survived unchanged to modern times and appear today in very mundane contexts. You will find, in fact, that the Tarot system itself is constructed and works in exactly the same way as the one you use every day, the only difference being in type, quality and quantity of information conveyed. The reason for this difference is obvious: a Tarot card is not a single sign or symbol designed to convey a single simple concept like 'Stop!', but a multiplicity of signs and symbols used in conjunction to convey an extremely complex concept in all its ramifications.

Like the contemporary system, the Tarot is 'reinforced' with regular letter alphabet symbols. Unlike the contemporary system, however, the Tarot is also 'reinforced' with three other sign/symbol genres (Number, Colour and Archetypal Images) and a foreign pure symbol system (Hebrew Letters).

The first of these, number, is extremely important, and is also closely associated with the foreign pure symbol system Hebrew letters. Numbers qualify as signs, ideographs and pure symbols; and Pythagoras put forward the theory that nothing in the universe could exist without them. Certainly they are not the simple indicators of quantity that they might appear to be — hence their long association with the sacred, and the development (some 10,000 years ago according to actual recorded evidence) of the science of Numerology, of which there are several systems now extant, all of which allot quite precise and defined meanings to numbers. Insofar as the Tarot is concerned, it is important to remember that the number that appears on each card is quite capable of expressing the entire concept portrayed as a picture on the card *purely symbolically*.

Hebrew letters can be associated with numbers because they *are* numbers.

There are twenty-two Hebrew letters altogether, each one of which is associated with one of the cards of the Major Arcana; and those twenty-two letters can be divided into three groups:

1. Mother Letters
2. Double Letters
3. Single Letters

There are three Mother letters: Aleph, Mem and Shin; seven Double letters: Beth, Gimel, Daleth, Kaph, Peh, Resh and Tau; and twelve Single letters: Heh, Vau, Zayin, Cheth, Teth, Yod, Lamed, Nun, Samekh, Ayin, Tzaddi and Qoph.

The three Mother letters are attributed to the three Elements that are taken into account in the Major Arcana, i.e.:

Aleph is attributed to Air
Mem is attributed to Water
Shin is attributed to Fire

The seven Double letters are attributed to the seven Planets, and are also considered to represent pairs of opposites, so:

Beth is attributed to Mercury — Life/Death
Gimel is attributed to the Moon — Wisdom/Folly
Daleth is attributed to Venus — Peace/War
Kaph is attributed to Jupiter — Riches/Poverty
Peh is attributed to Mars — Grace/Indignation
Resh is attributed to the Sun — Fertility/Barrenness
Tau is attributed to the World — Power/Servitude

The remaining twelve Single letters are, of course, attributed to the twelve signs of the Zodiac, so:

Heh is attributed to Aries
Vau is attributed to Taurus
Zayin is attributed to Gemini
Cheth is attributed to Cancer
Teth is attributed to Leo
Yod is attributed to Virgo
Lamed is attributed to Libra
Nun is attributed to Scorpio
Samekh is attributed to Sagittarius
Ayin is attributed to Capricorn
Tzaddi is attributed to Aquarius
Qoph is attributed to Pisces

You will see these attributions as you work your way through the sections dealing with the divinatory meanings of the cards of the Major Arcana, and should make an effort to learn them as you go along, for they are very important.

In addition, each of the twenty-two symbols that form the letters of the Hebrew alphabet represent three quite different things:

1. A letter of the Alphabet
2. A word in the Hebrew Language
3. A number

Thus the first symbol, Aleph, is:

1. A letter of the Alphabet corresponding to the English letter 'A'.

2. A word in the Hebrew language, Aleph, which means 'Ox'.
3. The number 1.

The rest of the numerical equivalents of the Hebrew Letters appear on the Table on page 121 and you should make an effort to learn these too eventually.

In that regard, you will notice that five of those letters: Kaph, Mem, Nun, Peh and Tzaddi have an extra number next to them on the list, and this is the number that is allotted to the final form of the letter, i.e., the form that is used when one of those letters forms the final letter of a word. This is a point of grammar that is particularly important to the Qabalist, whose work inevitably eventually involves working with Qabalistic Numerology.

The differing aspects of the Hebrew alphabet can be used in various ways, i.e.,

1. When a letter is used as a *word* and split into its component glyphs:
   Aleph = A(Aleph)/L(Lamed)/P(Peh)

the separate glyphs may be analysed as to their individual meanings, and those meanings related back to the original word. Thus the words Ox (Aleph), Whip (Lamed) and Mouth (Peh), can all be said to relate in some way to the card The Fool, to which the letter Aleph is attributed. Consequently, examination of the cards Justice (Lamed) and The Tower (Peh) will reveal some new aspect of the card The Fool, and also an interrelationship between all three cards. You will see from the Table on page 121 that the individual glyphs that make up each Hebrew letter are printed next to the letter itself, which will enable you to make these comparisons for yourself.

2. Because the letters of the Hebrew alphabet are also numbers, each letter/word of the alphabet may be written numerically. Consequently, the letter Aleph becomes:

i) Aleph (letter) = 1
ii) Aleph (word) = Aleph (1) + Lamed (30) + Peh (80)

The capability of Hebrew letters to be used as numbers in this way may be used to work the word/number sciences in Qabalistic Numerology, but this is advanced work, which is best ignored for the present.

Colour, the second on the list of symbol genres associated with the Tarot, qualifies as *pure symbol*, and it is unfortunate and surprising that the science of colour is so neglected in the modern world, since its physical and psychological effects are quite well known and could be used very beneficially in schools, hospitals and workplaces. As matters stand, however, colour is not utilized as it should be, and most people consequently have a very limited or confused knowledge of its symbology and uses.

Colour is an important factor in the Tarot because of its effects upon consciousness and its connection with resonance; but the interrelationship that exists between colour and sound is a rather complex one.

Sound is an atmospheric vibration. Colour is reflected light. The connecting link between these two things is a similar *vibratory rate*.

Standard pitch is the sound called 'Middle C'. Middle C has the vibratory rate of 256 vibrations per second, and we hear Middle C by the effect of those vibrations upon the ear, and the activity of the sound-centre of the brain.

If the number 256 (note, number again!) is doubled often enough, the note 'C' goes up through the musical scale until it is beyond the limits of human hearing; but that does not mean, of course, that it simply ceases to exist. Repeated doublings of the number will continue to symbolize whole series of 'Cs' until finally the vibratory rate corresponds to that of light, which is the vehicle of colour. Consequently, if the number 256 is doubled often enough, one comes to the exact number of vibrations per second which causes the sight centre, through the human eye, to perceive the colour 'red'.

Every semi-tone of the musical scale can be treated in this way, and the result is a scale of colours which correspond to musical notes. The Table on page 121 shows the colours and sounds that are associated with the cards of the Major Arcana, but for the time being, an afternoon spent with the *Lüscher Colour Test* — the abridged paperback version — will give you all the information you presently need regarding colour, and a chance to test the validity of current theories regarding human reaction to colour.

Archetypal Figures are the last of the symbol genres associated with the Tarot, and these represent *Cosmic Forces*, the vast network of stresses that are the building blocks of the universe and everything in it. Archetypal Images are symbols and pictographs, but they are rather different from the symbols we have dealt with so far, for although all symbols operate on levels other than a purely conscious one (and this accounts for the speed of our reactions to symbols as against our reaction speed to the same concept spelled out in words) this is particularly true of the Archetypal symbol genre.

The word 'archetype' means a pattern or model of which things of the same type are representations or copies; and Archetypal Figures are psychological models or patterns that exist in the consciousness of every individual, and derive from the experiences and belief structure of the race to which that individual belongs. Thus, to a very large extent they determine his reactions to people, situations and events. We all have an innate understanding and recognition of these figures, which are to a very large extent the result of mans' efforts to reduce the infinite and incomprehensible structures of the Universe

— and his own psyche — to more manageable intellectual levels by *humanizing* and *personalizing* them.*

The value of Archetypal Images as they appear in the Tarot lies in their ability to remind the user of knowledge and understanding that is pre-existing in his consciousness, but of which he is often unaware, and bring it through into normal consciousness. Obviously, a knowledge of myths and legends — which explain in story-form the same forces that Archetypal Images present pictorially — assists in this process considerably, which is why you have been asked to read some mythology in connection with your Tarot studies. This is particularly important, because of all the symbols used in the Tarot, Archetypal Images are the most essential. In fact they are the *raison d'être* of the Tarot, all other symbol genres being simply 'reinforcement tools' which serve only to reveal various aspects of the single central concept represented by Archetypal Images.

To illustrate how the various symbol genres work together in the Tarot to express a given concept, the genres that make up the Major Arcana card The Empress appear below isolated from their usual context so that they may be examined individually. The card used in this exercise is taken from the Rider-Waite Deck — the Deck you were advised to use at the beginning of this book. This Deck is the most commercial and readily available of all Tarot Decks and was drawn by Pamela Coleman Smith to Dr Arthur Edward Waite's specifications, *circa* 1909. The complete card appears opposite, labelled Card 'A'.

Beginning at the top of the card, the first thing to meet the eye is the Roman numeral III. The number 3 in this context has both an exoteric and an esoteric meaning. Exoterically, it is simply the face number of the card, and serves to place the card within the Deck as a whole. Esoterically, however, it represents the simplest manifestation of form or shape — the triangle; as well as the concept of self-expression. The number 3 resolves the tension that is inherent in the duality of the numbers 1 and 2; and is the number of creation, birth and fruitfulness.

---

* The trick of rendering abstracts comprehensible in this way has persisted to the present day, and is used extensively in advertising. The West Midlands Transport Company has devised this little fellow:

as a personification of its corporate identity; and there is presently a whole set of products in the United States bearing the portrait of a smiling globule called 'Little Herpie', underneath which appears the legend: 'Look Before You Sleep'. This has appeared in response to the epidemic of genital herpes, but in this case the smiling little personification is not a very good fit for the concept it represents!

Card 'A'

The next most obvious thing about the card is the figure of the woman seated in the centre of it. This is the Archetypal Figure, and represents the Great Mother (close examination of the card reveals that the figure is pregnant), or woman in her fruitful, life-giving aspect.

Most of the other symbols of the card are scattered on or around this central figure, reinforcing the concept it is intended to convey, for example:

1. *The Wreath and Crown of Stars*
   The wreath is made of myrtle, a plant sacred to Venus, who is a mother goddess as well as the goddess of love. The crown of twelve stars symbolizes the Zodiac, time, and dominion over the macrocosm.

2. *The Necklace*
   The necklace is made of seven pearls, which are Venusian, as are the pomegranates with their incorporated Astrological sigil ♀ which form the basis of the design on the Empress' gown. This same Astrological sigil

is repeated on the cushions against which the Empress is leaning, and yet again on the heart-shaped shield at her feet.

3. *The Sceptre and Globe*
   In her right hand, the Empress carries a sceptre mounted by a globe, representing dominion over material conditions.

4. *The Landscape*
   The figure is seated out of doors. The trees in the background of the picture are Cyprus trees, which are sacred to Venus. In the foreground is a patch of ripening wheat, which is sacred to Ceres, another mother goddess.

   The stream and pool reinforce the concept conveyed by the number 3 — the reconciliation of the duality inherent in the numbers 1 (the stream — masculine, formless, positive and active energy) and 2 (the pool — feminine, negative, passive, form-making energy).

At the foot of the card, the words: 'The Empress' constitute the last of the symbols of this card. These words, literally translated, mean: 'she who sets in order' — another reference to the form-making capabilities of feminine energy. In more earthly terms, of course, an Empress is the supreme woman of the land she inhabits.

Thus the general concept of this card can be seen to be birth (and so death also, for without birth there is no death), the coming into form or manifestation, and the creation of shape and order out of formlessness.

Obviously, different Tarot designers use different symbols to convey the same concepts — the number of symbols available for use is very large, and personal preference plays a large part in the choice of symbols used. The card illustrated opposite and labelled Card 'B' highlights some of these differences. It is taken from a Deck drawn by David Sheridan in 1972 specifically to illustrate Alfred Douglas' book *The Tarot* — so there was a time-lapse of almost three-quarters of a century between the appearance of the Waite Deck and this one. The Sheridan Deck is vividly coloured — too much so for some people, although I find it attractive and frequently work with it — and the symbology has been very much simplified and, in some cases, completely altered, many of the Waite symbols being absent, one having been replaced.

The necklace, sceptre and globe, for instance, have all been omitted, as have the decorations on the Empress' gown. The field of wheat that appeared on the Waite card has been replaced with a single ear of wheat which is held in the Empress' right hand. The myrtle wreath, Cyprus trees, stream and pool are all much less clearly delineated; and while the shield remains, the Astrological sigil of Venus which figured on the shield in the Waite version has been replaced by the stylized form of a dove. This bird is sacred to Venus, and is also a symbol of the Holy Spirit. Enclosed thus in the shield it is a reminder of the spirit that is enclosed within all envelopes of form, and so is a very acceptable alternative symbol. The twelve stars about the Empress' head

Card 'B'

remain, but their positioning now suggests a halo rather than a crown. A cornucopia — symbol of everlasting abundance and plenty — has been added, replacing the sigil covered cushions and couch of the Waite design; and a Sun in Splendour has also been added, signifying the original current of creative force behind the whole.

When the various symbols that go to make up a single card are reviewed in this way, a pattern emerges which reveals the basic content of the complete card, *but not its complete meaning*. Thus, to review the symbols of which the Tarot is constructed in this purely intellectual way can be equated with 'skimming' through a book — you get the general outline, but not the details of the story.

Unfortunately, it is beyond the scope of a book of this kind to provide a symbol review section for you, just as it is not possible to provide you with even a brief synopsis of the meaning of numbers, and the finer points of colourology, because all these subjects require a book to themselves. I would, however, urge you to either buy or borrow three books to be read in conjunction with this one — Paul Foster Case's *The Tarot* which provides an excellent symbol review of the cards; Paul Avery's *The Numbers of Life* which provides an excellent overview of both Qabalistic and Pythagorean Numerology; and the previously mentioned *Lüscher Colour Test* — because at the beginning of your work with the Tarot a general outline of the symbology involved is very important indeed to your progress.

Needless to say, if you do obtain the books as I suggest, you need not commence the entire programme of learning immediately — just as you need not learn by heart the attributions listed in this Chapter immediately — but you would be well advised to commence on it (and thereafter commence to improve on it by way of meditation, which we shall be discussing at some length in the next Chapter) *before* you commence on Part Two of this book.

Tarot Attributions

Hebrew Letter	Syllables	Numerical Equivalents	Colour	Sound	Tarot Card	Astrological Symbol
ALEPH	ALP	1	Bright pale yellow	E	The Fool	◁ Air
BETH	BITh	2	Yellow	E	The Magician	☿ Mercury
GIMEL	GML	3	Blue	G	The Papess	☽ The Moon
DALETH	DLTh	4	Emerald Green	F	The Empress	♀ Venus
HEH	HH	5	Scarlet	C	The Emperor	♈ Aries
VAU	VV	6	Red-Orange	C	The Pope	♉ Taurus
ZAIN	ZIN	7	Orange	D	The Lovers	♊ Gemini
CHETH	ChITh	8	Amber	D	The Chariot	♋ Cancer
TETH	TITh	9	Greenish Yellow	E	Strength	♌ Leo
YOD	YUD	10	Yellowish Green	F	The Hermit	♍ Virgo
KAPH	KP	20 (500)	Violet	A	The Wheel of Fortune	♃ Jupiter
LAMED	LMD	30	Emerald Green	F	Justice	♎ Libra
MEM	MIM	40 (600)	Deep Blue	G	The Hanged Man	▽ Water
NUN	NUN	50 (700)	Green Blue	G	Death	♏ Scorpio
SAMEKH	SMK	60	Blue	G	Temperance	♐ Sagittarius
AYIN	OIN	70	Indigo	A	The Devil	♑ Capricorn
PEH	PH	80 (800)	Scarlet	C	The Tower	♂ Mars
TZADDI	TzDI	90 (900)	Violet	A	The Star	♒ Aquarius
QOPH	QUP	100	Crimson	B	The Moon	♓ Pisces
RESH	RISh	200	Orange	D	The Sun	☉ The Sun
SHIN	ShIN	300	Orange Scarlet	C	Judgement	△ Fire
TAU	ThU	400	Indigo	A	The World	♄ Saturn

The Fool

The Spirit of the Aether

Card Number: 0
Key Number: 11
Rulership: Air
Hebrew Letter: Aleph
Translation: Ox
Numerical Value: 3

Dignified:	The beginning of a new life-cycle and all new beginnings. Energy, optimism, happiness and force. Circumstances and occurrences that are unexpected and unplanned, and which overturn existing states. Important decisions and choices to be made.
Ill-Dignified:	Reckless or impulsive action and choices. Folly and indiscretion. The frittering away or waste of creative energy. Sometimes indicates an individual who starts many new things but finishes nothing and who consistently seeks change of environment or job.
Mythological Note:	Zeus. Jupiter. Hoor-Paar-Kraat, Lord of Silence.

The Magician

The Magus of Power

Card Number: 1
Key Number: 12
Ruleship: Mercury
Hebrew Letter: Beth
Translation: House
Numerical Value: 9

Dignified: Will, mastery, skill and oratory. Initiative and a willingness to take risks. An ability to perceive and utilize one's own potential. Organizational and communicatory skills.

Ill-Dignified: Timidity. Hesitation. Shyness. Indecision. Self-depreciation. A poor self image. An inability to utilize time or talents properly. Difficulty of self-expression. Hesitation of speech, poor co-ordination and learning disabilities, sometimes.

Mythological
Note: Hermes, god of wisdom and magic. Mercury, god of wisdom and magic. Thoth, god of magic and writing. Odin the wanderer and inventor of poetry and runes. All gods that are planners and arrangers of life, rather than makers of it.

The Papess

The Priestess of the Silver Star

Card Number: 2
Key Number: 13
Rulership: The Moon ☽
Hebrew Letter: Gimel
Translation: Camel
Numerical Value: 9

Dignified: Intuitive insight suggests new solutions. The influence of women. Hidden influences at work and in the home. Mysteries and secrets. Hidden influences from the psyche affect personal circumstances.

Ill-Dignified: Problems resulting from a lack of foresight. In women, an inability to understand or come to terms with themselves or other women. Surface or facile knowledge. Self conceit sometimes. In men an unwillingness to accept that part of themselves which is feminine.

Mythological
Note: Artemis, the huntress. Hecate. All Moon goddesses.

The Empress

The Daughter of the Mighty Ones

Card Number: 3
Key Number: 14
Rulership: Venus   ♀
Hebrew Letter: Daleth
Translation: Door
Numerical Value: 9

Dignified:	Fertility, abundance and material wealth. Domestic stability and maternal care. Creativity in all things, and, dependent upon surrounding cards, security and growth. Marriage and pregnancy sometimes and depending on other cards.
Ill-Dignified:	Domestic upheaval. Sterility and unwanted pregnancy sometimes. Poverty sometimes. Stifled or 'blocked' creativity often. Infertility or promiscuity.
Mythological Note:	Venus. Aphrodite. Hathor. Freyja. All goddesses of love. All goddesses of agriculture. All gods/goddesses portraying the attraction of the positive for the negative.

The Emperor

Son of the Morning; Chief among the Mighty

Card Number: 4
Key Number: 15
Rulership: Aries   ♈
Hebrew Letter: Heh   ה
Translation: Window
Numerical Value: 12

Dignified:	Governmental and corporate identities. Temporal power. Authority. Leadership. Will power. Self-control acquired through experience. Powerful individuals or entities.
Ill-Dignified:	A dislike of authority, corporate, governmental or parental. An inability to deal with authority, or a contempt for order of that kind. An inability to command oneself or others. Loss or lack of ambition. Immaturity. Possible bondage to a parent or parental figure.
Mythological Note:	Athena as protectress of the state. Minerva as goddess of war. Mentu as god of war. Tyr as god of courage and valour and honour in war. Mars as god of war.

The Pope

The Magus of the Eternal

Card Number: 5
Key Number: 16
Rulership: Taurus ♉
Hebrew Letter: Vau
Translation: Nail
Numerical Value: 12

Dignified: Good counsel, advice and teaching. A seeker after knowledge and wisdom. A preference for the orthodox and a need to conform — to be socially acceptable. Strict adherence to religion, sometimes. Marriage sometimes.

Ill-Dignified: Slander, propaganda and bad advice. Misrepresentation in the advertisement or sale of goods. Unconventionality. Distortion of truth.

Mythological
Note: Bacchus. Christ in Olympus. Parsival as King-Priest. Apis. Hera, goddess of marriage. Hymen, god of marriage. Dionysius. All gods of redemption.

Instructions for the Astrological Spread

1. Place the Significator in a central position, and then deal 12 cards from the top of the Deck as per the diagram opposite.
2. Read each card singly and having reference to the Key to the Astrological Spread below; i.e., the card in position 1 will have reference to the Querent's disposition and current problems, and so on.

Because one single card will not supply in-depth information about any given aspect of the Querent's life, it is often best to deal four cards or more into each of the twelve positions — and these cards may be dealt in blocks of four or more, or singly and following the pattern, as desired.

Key to the Astrological Spread

Card 1 — Aries   — Represents the Querent, his disposition and his current problems.
Card 2 — Taurus   — Represents the Querent's financial situation.
Card 3 — Gemini   — Represents travel and communication.
Card 4 — Cancer   — Represents the Querent's home life, his siblings and his parents.
Card 5 — Leo   — Represents the Querent's pleasures.
Card 6 — Virgo   — Represents the Querent's health.
Card 7 — Libra   — Represents partnerships and marriages.
Card 8 — Scorpio   — Represents inheritances and deaths.
Card 9 — Sagittarius — Represents philosophy, religion, education and dreams.
Card 10 — Capricorn   — Represents the Querent's career.
Card 11 — Aquarius   — Represents the Querent's friends.
Card 12 — Pisces   — Represents the Querent's burdens, restrictions, and secret fears.

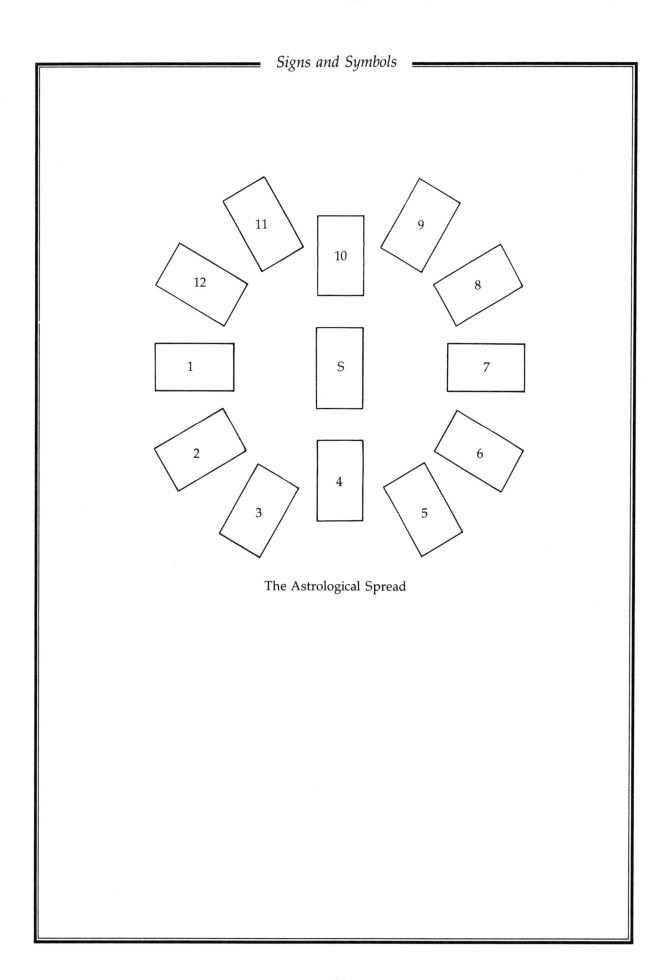

The Astrological Spread

10.

Meditation . . .

Learning to recognize and appreciate the symbol content of the Tarot on an intellectual level is only the first step toward achieving a genuine understanding of it; for the subtle 'picture language' of the Deck is the language of the intuitive unconscious rather than the logical conscious mind, and must be appreciated on that level if it is to be properly appreciated at all.

Such an appreciation is best achieved by a process called **Meditation**, because the unconscious cannot be approached direct by the egocentric conscious mind, but only circuitously, by way of the symbols that are its own language, and when the clamour of everyday consciousness has been deliberately quieted.

Meditation is a special kind of concentration, the purpose of which is to withdraw all the energy — physical, mental and emotional — that is usually expended upon multiple external factors, and turn it inward to examine a single predetermined concept.

This sounds as if it should be a very simple process — and, indeed, it should be — but it is not; and there are two reasons for this.

Firstly, the mind of the average person is not used to functioning in this way — and will show no disposition to readily get used to it either; for the mind of the average person is very lazy, and the singleminded concentration demanded by meditation constitutes much harder work than that to which it is accustomed.

Secondly, the process of turning the mind inward upon itself causes channels to be opened between the conscious and the unconscious minds, often with unpleasant repercussions.

These repercussions occur simply because it is one of the functions of the unconscious mind to act as the storehouse of personal memory and experience.

This means, of course, that actions and reactions, words and feelings — experiences long forgotten on a conscious level — are all recorded in the personal unconscious in minute detail, and can be brought forth in their entirety once the barrier of consciousness that normally restrains the freedom of expression of the personal unconscious is released.

Unfortunately, the contents of the personal unconscious are never wholly pleasant, since among the accumulated record of the life experiences there will exist some that have been repressed or deliberately 'forgotten', on a conscious level, because they are unpleasant or painful.

Consequently, although even a very small degree of conscious contact with the unconscious mind via the technique of meditation can prove very beneficial, and can often logically explain (and therefore put an end to) some of the seemingly illogical and arbitrary reactions and fears that plague and sometimes seriously distort our lives; such contact may prove difficult to achieve or sustain, because repeated access to the unconscious inevitably results sooner or later in the rediscovery of old psychic wounds, which prove to be as fresh, as painful and as unpleasant in retrospect as they were when they were first inflicted.

Often, therefore, when meditation is first attempted, a battle of wits and wills ensues between the meditator and himself in the person of his own mind; for the mind will strive to evade both the unaccustomed control and hard work that is demanded by the technique, and will shy away as well from the pain of memory and the possibility of further pain that memory entails.

This is a battle that can only be won by perseverance: for only if the niggling urge *not* to meditate — or to put it off until the tomorrow that never comes — is consistently ignored, and the mind persistently made to conform to the will, can a truce with oneself (and, eventually, a victory over oneself), ever be achieved.

The unconscious, however, is not just a personal and detailed diary record of the events of our lives. It is also the connecting link between the conscious mind (or us as self-conscious individuals) and the Universal Unconscious (or us as part of the universal life stream).

This means that a degree of conscious contact with our own unconscious can also give us access to the entire accumulated body of the Universal Unconscious, which retains details of the universal experience in exactly the same way as our own personal unconscious retains details of experiences personal to us.

There are, therefore, definite and lasting benefits to be had from perseverance with the technique of meditation; for, firstly, during successful meditation, the mind begins to operate at a much higher level of precision and clarity, and the body relaxes, its functions becoming slow and rhythmic — and both body and mind retain a certain degree of these qualities permanently if meditation is undertaken regularly.

Consequently, and on a very mundane level, regular meditators show improved concentration; improved ability to think logically; and the physically beneficial results of complete, thorough and regular relaxation of the body.

In addition, the expanded consciousness that is the most well-known effect of meditation, allied with realizations* with regard to the concepts examined

---

* The word 'realization' in this context meaning knowledge that is understood rather than simply learned.

in meditation, leads regular meditators toward a greater understanding of themselves generally and as spiritual beings; and they thus cease to suffer — as most of us do at some time or another — from the feeling that life is futile or meaningless.

Finally, of course, it is facts plucked from the stream of the Universal Unconscious — where all that was, is, and will be, is known; and where time has a different structure from that to which we are more usually accustomed* — that supply the material of which 'psychic' readings are made.

Meditation is a technique common to all occult systems; indeed, the necessity of meditation to the enhancement of health, spiritual growth and understanding is the one (and almost the only) point upon which all occultists of every type and description can be guaranteed categorically to agree; but most of the readily available information on the subject relates to Eastern rather than Western techniques.

This is a pity, because although the two systems complement each other, and both have the identical aim of the liberation of the true self, there is little doubt that Eastern occult systems are better suited to Eastern, rather than Western, minds and bodies. The two systems are in any event diametrically opposed in method.

Eastern occult systems, for example, are passive and primarily mystical. They rely upon the use of meditation allied with *mantras* (or words which must be repeated/vibrated, over and over again) and *mandalas* (symbolic pictures or designs), to effectively distract the mind from external sensory stimuli and concentrate it on the desired single point. Eastern systems aim at the *suppression* of the mind, body and will, so that the true self may appreciate its distinction from them and so obtain liberation.

Western systems, on the other hand, are active and primarily magical, i.e., they use *ritual* as well as mandalas, mantras and meditation, to concentrate and channel the activity of the mind. Western systems aim at *control* of the body and mind and *activation* of the will so that the true self can be integrated into the personality, which will thus be a reflection of it.

Most importantly of all, however, Eastern systems of meditation are designed to react directly upon the physical body, while Western ones are not; and this means that although the side effects** of the two systems are the same, the mode of progression toward the desired goal is very different.

Consequently, the two systems can never be used in conjunction with any degree of safety, i.e., you cannot use a Western mandala with an Eastern

---

* See Chapter 12, 'Dimensions'.

** Which include, but are not limited to, increased control over personal environment; greatly expanded psychic awareness, and enhanced true individuation.

system of meditation (or vice-versa).*

This is a very important point; since due to the widespread availability of books, films and lectures that approach the subject from an Eastern standpoint, and the high visibility generally of Eastern occultists and their techniques — as opposed to the characteristically low profile and almost paranoid secrecy that is still adopted (wisely or not) by their Western counterparts — if you have been exposed to any system of meditation at all it is probably an Eastern one.

If this is so, it is very important indeed that you understand that it will not be possible for you to use such a meditation technique in conjunction with an occult tool so fundamentally Western in nature as the Tarot; and that if you want to undertake Tarot meditation at all (and this is advisable if you want to get the best out of yourself and your cards) then you will have to undertake to learn a Western system of meditation as well.

Fortunately, this is not a difficult proposition, for Western techniques of meditation do not involve the time or effort demanded by most of their Eastern counterparts, and can be learned with comparative ease — which does *not* mean, of course, that these techniques are less effective or less efficient; but only that they are *different*, having been devised for Western minds, bodies, and lifestyles rather than Eastern ones.

All Western occult techniques, in fact, are designed for 'doers': busy people leading busy lives in busy places; and Western meditation techniques are no exception. They are not, as many of their Eastern counterparts are, designed for the use of people who live 'out of the world', and who therefore have a great deal of time at their disposal.

Indeed, the concept of 'cutting oneself off' from reality; of giving up actual work in the commonplace world to concentrate entirely upon things of the spirit, is one that is actively frowned upon in the Western Tradition, which advocates that moderation and balance be maintained in all things.

Consequently, the meditation techniques of the Western Tradition are less involved, take less time, and demand neither perfection of posture nor any particular physical attitude at all, the yardstick by which successful meditation is judged being the same one by which the success of any venture is judged in the West — results obtained.

Naturally, of course, the system must be approached carefully and in an orderly manner; and the rule of thumb here is that meditation is best and most

---

* In fact it is perfectly possible to use, say, Hatha Yoga asanas and postures with Western mandalas, but *not* the associated Ida and Pingala breathing techniques, because these are designed to react directly upon the physical body — and are consequently unsafe for use with mandalas designed to react on very different levels, as the Tarot images are.

Since it is difficult to 'split' a technique in this way once it has been learned, however, i.e., to use some portions of a technique and discard others, it is safer to discard the method entirely and learn a new one that properly fits its intended purpose.

productive when undertaken regularly for short periods every day — 10 to 15 minutes well spent and persevered with — at the same time of day, and following a pre-arranged and strictly adhered to curriculum of work.

Usually, such a curriculum is constructed by the Director or other personnel of an occult school — for normally it is only persons who have been or are working under the direction of such a school who practise Western techniques of meditation seriously at all.

Since you are already working with the Tarot, however, you need neither join such a school (which would not suit at least 80 per cent of you), nor go to the trouble of constructing a curriculum for yourself; because the Major Arcana (which in any event forms the curriculum upon which most such schools work) constitutes in and of itself an ideal pre-constructed curriculum package that could keep you busy for many years.

There are some simple instructions and exercises for meditation at the end of this chapter; and you should undertake to complete those exercises daily for at least one week before progressing further, because these exercises are preparatory ones, and if you do not complete them, you will not be able to complete the other, and more interesting meditation exercises that appear at the end of the next chapter and in Part Two of this book.

It is not necessary — in fact it is not a very good idea — to complete the meditation exercises given with this chapter before you complete your fantasy plays and Practice Spread; and you should not neglect your ordinary 'reading practice' so as to devote more time or attention to the new exercises that are coming your way. The practice exercises may be completed — once a day for at least one week — at a time most convenient to yourself, and should at most absorb twenty minutes of your time. Any other 'learning time' you have left over during the week should be devoted to ordinary 'reading practice', and in this regard you might now want to begin to incorporate the **combinations** factor into your readings.

Combinations are used to give meanings to groups of cards of the same face number that appear within a single Spread — three of the four fours for instance, or three of the fives. This occurs quite often, and can give you just that little bit of extra information that clarifies the entire Spread, so it is well worth the trouble of (I'm afraid!) the rote learning involved.

The combinations involved are as follows:

Aces
4 — Great power or force
3 — Riches and success
2 — Change of place — residence or work

Twos
4 — Conferences and conversation
3 — Reorganization

Threes
4 — Resolution and determination
3 — Deceit

Fours
4 — Rest and peace
3 — Industry and industriousness

Fives
4 — Quarrels and fights
3 — Order and regularity

Sixes
4 — Peace
3 — Gain and success

Sevens
4 — Disappointment
3 — Contracts

Eights
4 — Much news
3 — Much travelling

Nines
4 — Added responsibilities
3 — Correspondence

Tens
4 — Anxiety and responsibility
3 — Buying, selling and commerce

Knaves
4 — Schools and colleges, education, new plans and new ideas
3 — Children in groups
2 — Play, fun and sporting events

Knights
4 — Armed forces or dominant clique. Swiftness and rapidity of action
3 — Groups of people. Parties or celebrations
2 — Old Friends from the past

Queens
4 — Local or city government
3 — Groups of women. Clubs. Powerful friends
2 — Gossip or slander

Kings
4 — State or world government. Meetings of the great
3 — Fraternal organizations or lodges. Groups of men. Fashion
2 — Business opportunities

The Lovers

The Children of the Voice; the Oracle of the Mighty Gods

Card Number: 6
Key Number: 17
Rulership: Gemini   Ⅱ
Hebrew Letter: Zain
Translation: A Sword or
                 Weapon
Numerical Value: 12

Dignified: Choice to be made intuitively rather than intellectually. Inspiration. Hunches. Second sight. Abstract thought. True partnerships. Internal harmony.

Ill-Dignified: Contradiction. Duality. Conflict with self. A partnership disrupted by external factors.

Mythological
Note: Castor and Pollux. Rekht and Merti. Apollo as the diviner. Janus of the two faces. Hoor-Paar-Kraat who contains within himself the twin gods Horus and Harpocrates, Lords of Strength and Silence respectively.

The Chariot

The Child of the Powers of the Waters; the Lord of the Triumph of Light

Card Number: 7
Key Number: 18
Rulership: Cancer
Hebrew Letter: Cheth
Translation: A Fenced
                   or
                   Enclosed
                   Field
Numerical Value: 12

Dignified: Self-control. Self-confidence. Mastery of external factors. Will-power. Triumph over life's obstacles. Success as a result of effort, and not fortune. The careful building up of a successful existence within the bounds set by the conditions of life.

Ill-Dignified: Imbalance. Destruction. Loss of control under pressure of external circumstances due to flaws of character. The maintenance of outworn traditions and ideas. Self limitation.

Mythological Note: Hermod, the envoy of the gods. Mercury as messenger of the gods. Apollo as charioteer.

Strength (Fortitude)

The Daughter of the Flaming Sword

Card Number: 8
Key Number: 19
Rulership: Leo   ♌
Hebrew Letter: Teth
Translation: Serpent
Numerical Value: 12

Dignified: Courage. Strength. The synergic interaction of mental and emotional forces. Control of passion and defeat of base impulses. An arbitrator sometimes.

Ill-Dignified: Weakness. Defeat. Concession. Self-indulgence. Lack of self-discipline and surrender to unworthy impulse. A clash of interests sometimes.

Mythological
Note: Pasht. Sekket. Mau. All cat goddesses. Ra Hoor Kruit as god of the Sun (which rules Leo). Demeter and Venus as agricultural goddesses.

The Hermit

The Prophet of the Eternal; the Magus of the Voice of Power

Card Number: 9
Key Number: 20
Rulership: Virgo ♍
Hebrew Letter: Yod ‎י
Translation: The Human
                  Hand,
                  Closed to
                  Grasp or
                  Hold
Numerical Value: 12

Dignified: Prudence. Planning. Forethought. Foresight. Counsel sought and taken. A warning against precipitous action or thought. An indication that there is a need to retire or disassociate oneself from activity in order to think and evaluate circumstances.

Ill-Dignified: Counsel or assistance refused. Reliance on one's own inadequate resources. Groundless suspicion of the motives of others. Obstinate continuance of bad habits or unproductive lifestyles.

Mythological
Note: Isis and Nephthys as virgin goddesses. Narcissus who was inaccessible to the emotion of love. Adonis. Balder as virgin god.

The Wheel of Fortune
The Lord of the
Forces of Life

Card Number: 10
Key Number: 21
Rulership: Jupiter
Hebrew Letter: Kaph
Translation: Hand
Numerical Value: 9

Dignified:	Change of fortune. The beginning of a new cycle. Progress. Advancement. Improvement. The card of good fortune and Karmic change.
Ill-Dignified:	As above, but in the longer term. Resistance of change which is inevitable sometimes, and depending upon surrounding cards.
Mythological Note:	Pluto as the blind giver of wealth. Njord as the guardian of wealth. Jupiter and Zeus, expansive and beneficient bringers of good fortune.

Instructions for the Twenty-One Card Romany Spread

The Romany Spread is a good, simple Spread with clearly defined 'timing' parameters that works well when one is called upon to examine a single problem in depth. You should commence this Spread as follows:

1. Read and follow the instructions given in the Reader's Check List.

2. Deal twenty-one cards from the top of the Deck in the pattern shown below.

3. Read the top row of cards (i.e., cards numbered 1 through 7 on the diagram) first. These cards represent the past, and will therefore show the development of the matter at hand.

4. The second row of cards (i.e., those numbered 8 through 14 on the diagram) represent the present, and consequently show where matters stand.

5. The third and last row of cards will show future trends, and, possibly, an eventual outcome to the problem.

This Spread is particularly useful when the reading was commenced with a Spread designed to give an overall forecast, since it can be used to examine problems indicated in such an overall forecast in greater depth.

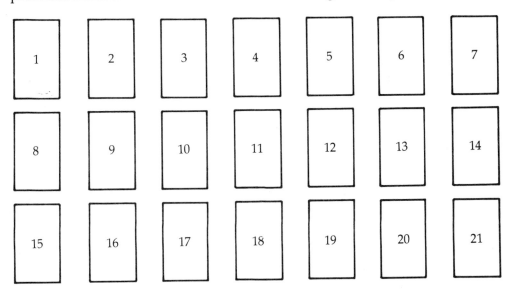

Twenty-One Card Romany Spread

Meditation Exercise

1. Begin by choosing one of the Major Arcana Cards that you have worked on to date.

2. Spend at least ten minutes 'mind's eye examining' the card you have chosen. Make sure that you can reproduce this card *in your mind*.

3. Test this by closing your eyes and seeing how much of the picture on the card you can reproduce in your mind.

4. Turn to the page that shows the divinatory meaning of the card you have chosen. Look at the Hebrew letter at the top of that page, and go through the same 'mind's eye examination' process with this letter. Test this by drawing the letter, and then reproducing it, with your eyes closed, *in your mind*.

5. Settle yourself comfortably in your armchair, with your feet together, and your hands in your lap. Then read the rest of this exercise through carefully, and when you are sure you are ready to begin, go on to the next point.

6. Having achieved a comfortable position, close your eyes, and make a deliberate effort to relax. Begin this relaxation process at your feet, and progress to your face and head. Breathe easily and naturally through your nose, and become aware of your breathing. You may, if you wish, say the word 'one', silently to yourself whenever you breathe out. If you become aware of noises in the room or in the street, make a deliberate effort not to think of them as annoyances, because this will only make them more intrusive. If you try to accept them, you will find that they are *not* intrusive at all.

7. When you feel that you are sufficiently relaxed; call up into your mind the image of the card that you have chosen, and see it *as a card*, that is; as a piece of pasteboard with a border and a picture on it hanging against a black background.

8. When you have fixed that image firmly in your mind; concentrate on it and it alone, and commence to draw the image closer, very slowly, so that the black background you imagined disappears, and the entire range of your mental vision is filled by the picture on the card, surrounded by its border.

9. When you have achieved this, you will find that you are facing a landscape through a kind of door. On the doorstep of that door will appear the name of the card you have chosen. It will look very large. On the lintel of the door, above your head, you will see the roman numeral of the card you have chosen — and this too will appear to be very large. At your sides, and within reach of your mental hands, will be the white door jam that is in reality the white border of the card.

10. What you must do next is likely to prove difficult at your first attempt, but will become much easier with practice; for you must now mentally step over the doorstep and into the landscape beyond it.

11. Once you have overcome the difficulty that is usually experienced at this point, you will find that you are free to wander in the landscape you have visualized and to adventure in it.

    You may also converse with the inhabitants of that landscape, and learn from them; for you will find that your attempt at creative visualization has indeed potentiated your imagination as it is supposed to do; and that both the landscape and its inhabitants will appear to be quite real. This is, of course, quite fascinating, but you should keep it always to the forefront of your mind that the experience is subjective and *not* objective.

12. Thereafter, it remains only to return — and this must be done correctly if it is to be done well and offer no unaccustomed shock to your system.

    Returning to normal consciousness should therefore *not* consist of suddenly opening your eyes and leaping out of your chair in a state of disorientation, but of completing the entire process outlined above in reverse.

13. This can be achieved in two ways. You can:
    a) Simply step backwards through your white doorway, seeing the card name reappear beneath your feet; or
    b) Practise your powers of visualization further by seeing the white doorway and, through it, the room in which you commenced this exercise.

    If you choose the latter method of returning to normal consciousness, you must see the room you left behind from the correct angle, i.e., you will be visualizing a portion of the room that is in reality behind you.

    Do not visualize yourself sitting in that room; not because it is in any way dangerous to do so, but because there is nothing more unnerving — at this point, in any event — than being made suddenly aware that you *can* be in two places at once.

14. When you have fully returned to normal consciousness and before you do anything else, you should write down a full description of your experiences, including what you saw, what you did, what you felt, and the gist of any conversation you may have had. This latter may prove difficult as it is notoriously hard to recall what is said in these situations; but you should at least try to remember and write down any fragments you can, however nonsensical these may appear to be. Practice makes perfect in this, as in everything else; and quite often phrases that seem very odd indeed when you write them down take on a certain sense when you look at them afterwards.

    Such realizations as you do obtain, of course, will be absolutely personal to you and have meaning in terms of your own psychic structure. They are intended to give you insight into your own personality; and in this regard you should be aware that such insights are sometimes unpleasant because they jog to the surface certain memories that you have very carefully forgotten. Perseverance, if this happens, is the only way to clear things up; and with perseverance — however unpleasant this might be — is the way you should proceed, for it is the only sure route to success.

Because realizations *are* personal and individual, and if you are working in a group, you will find that those of you who choose the same card will have very different realizations about it. This does not mean that somebody has gone wrong. On the contrary, it is worth listening to everybody's realizations about a single card because each individual's realization will simply be a facet of *a truth*, the single truth of which the card is an expression.

15. When you have written down all your realizations, you should ensure your full return to consciousness by getting up and doing *something*; even if it is only stamping your feet — which is, incidentally, the classic and accepted gesture with which to end a meditation session, because it symbolizes a very literal 'feet on the floor' return to the material world.

You should complete this exercise, with the same card, or with others that you have already dealt with in the chapter material, every day for the next seven days. Thereafter, if you like, you may incorporate this exercise into the following chapters, meditating on one card every day until you have completed an initial mediation on the entire Deck. If you do decide to follow this course, you would of course be best advised to take each card in order according to its face number, commencing with The Fool, and ending with The World, but this is not absolutely essential.

If you are working in a group, do share your meditation realizations with each other. Quite often, this leads to a very good understanding of the cards much more quickly than would be the case were you working alone, and had only your own meditation realizations to go by.

11.

... and Visualization

As part of the exercise to the previous chapter, you were asked to visualize certain things; and visualization is an essential part of meditation after the Western Tradition, which demands the development of the ability to visualize *creatively*.

Creative visualization is the term used to describe a technique designed to train the memory and imagination to reproduce, within the mind and in exact detail, objects, people and situations complete with the sights, sounds, smells and tactile sensations of reality.

This technique (which is basically creative daydreaming) is arguably the greatest and most important of all the occult arts. It is also one of the most difficult to master. This is because, for one thing, *exact* visualization, like total recall, comes naturally to very few people; as for most of us, acts of imagination of such magnitude are possible only after months or even years of consistent and patient practice.

Secondly, the imaginative faculty, which we all possess to an abundant degree as children, is quite often discouraged or actively repressed in most of us in our formative years, because it is thought to be an undesirable quality, that leads to the 'time wasting' activity of daydreaming. Consequently, we lose touch with our imaginative faculty almost completely at a very early age, and find it very difficult indeed to regain it on demand in later life.

The purpose of creative visualization in the Western Tradition is twofold. Firstly, it can be used in meditation to 'enliven' scenes such as those found on Tarot cards, thus potentiating the imagination and ensuring 'active' and enlightening meditation sessions. Alternatively, it may be used to create a scenario in the mind which it is intended should eventually come to take place in reality.

The first of these alternatives constitutes the primary use of the technique, and you are already — or at least you should be — quite familiar with it, for you have been using a modified form of it throughout this book to 'mind's eye examine' both your cards and the absent Querents for whom you have chosen to read.

The second alternative, however, is probably quite unfamiliar to you, and depends for its successful application upon the power of the human mind, working in concert with certain cosmic laws, to affect the plastic ether that underlies the reality we see about us every day, and so change it.

This latter is the most important — and the most misunderstood — use of the technique of creative visualization; and has, in modified form, been modernized and popularized (and rather poorly utilized) under the new title of 'positive thinking', although 'positive thinking' as it is presented by the various books and courses available on the subject is only a pale and barely recognizable shadow of its more powerful cousin, creative visualization.

This use of the technique of creative visualization is not, strictly speaking, germane to the purposes of this book; but we will nevertheless examine it in some detail here, for reasons which will shortly become clear.

The hows and whys of creative visualization, when it is used to 'tamper' with reality, can be very succinctly summed up by two well-known occult precepts, the first of which is *as above, so below*.

To understand the concept behind this rather cryptic phrase, which basically means that the macrocosm (or larger scheme of things) affects and can be affected by the microcosm (man), you must first appreciate that reality exists on many levels, and that those levels differ from one another, the level which we call reality being only the last, and the densest of many. These levels, which are separate from, and yet closely associated with, each other in time and space, together form a complex and closely interwoven matrix of being that is organized and purposeful, and that involves everything that is.

A more complete examination of these levels and their mode of operation is given both in Chapter 12 and in Part Two of this book; but insofar as we are concerned here, the most important thing to appreciate about them is that all events first occur on the highest of them — a level which is termed 'Archetypal' by occultists — and that the higher levels are more fluid and less dense than the lower ones.

Events that will eventually come into being on the material level — our reality — first exist on the Archetypal level, where they exist in essence, but not yet in fact — or rather, not yet in our material fact — and there is a slight lapse of time between the birth of any given event on the Archetypal, or highest level; its passage through the intervening levels; and its corresponding existence in our 'reality'.

This time lapse is very important, for it means, of course, that any event that occurs in our dense reality has already occurred, in essence, on a less dense, more plastic and higher cosmic level — on which level it can, if the task is approached correctly, be altered to a more desirable pattern.*

The morals of altering reality in this way we will examine shortly, but for the time being we will concentrate on its mechanics — the 'hows' of the situation as opposed to the 'whys' we have examined above. These are very well explained by the second of the two occult precepts mentioned earlier. i.e., 'thoughts are things.'

The truth of this statement can be very difficult to come to terms with, because we are used to thinking of things in a very material sense (tables, for example are 'things', as are telephones or walls or cars), or as being, in fact, tangible shapes.

Thoughts are not, of course, tangible on this, the material level, and they have no tangible shape here either; but they do have *a* shape, for theirs is the capability of defining shape, and they are the media whereby shape is given to concepts that would otherwise remain formless.

The capability of thought to define shape, however, is best illustrated not by reference to material objects like tables (which are, of course, fully capable of expression in material terms) but by reference to abstract concepts, or concepts that cannot be expressed in material terms but which nevertheless retain shape in the mind.

'Honour' for example, is just such an abstract, and patience is another; for although these 'things' can never be expressed as material objects, they are nevertheless states of being that have shape in the mind — and therefore existence also, for only when shape and expression are given to concepts can they have any existence at all.

There is a level within the matrix of being — it is not the Archetypal level, but it is nevertheless a level that is a good deal less dense than the one our physical bodies inhabit — upon which thoughts do not only define, but actually determine shape. Indeed, thoughts on that level are an active creative force capable of having the sort of direct impact upon the environment that they lack on this one. Thus thought can be said to have two basic capabilities within the cosmic scheme: it will *define* shape on this, the densest of the levels; and *determine* it on other, more subtle ones.

Consequently, it is possible to use concentrated thought and imaginative imagery — creative visualization, in other words — to change reality, or to

---

* If you find it difficult to imagine the course of events described above, it is often helpful to visualize the cosmic whole as a multi-layered trifle.

At the base of the trifle, there is a layer of sponge cake (which corresponds to our reality), on the top of which lie various layers of jelly, blancmange and fruit (which correspond to the intervening levels), the whole being topped with a layer of cream (which for our purposes will represent the Archetypal level).

If you then imagine the trifle being cut, and equate that with an event going through the cosmic system, you will see that the knife first touches the cream (Archetypal level), descends through the layers (intervening levels), and — after a short lapse of time — bites into the sponge cake which forms the bottom layer of the whole.

determine its shape; and this is done by deliberately directing thought to the correct level, where reality is more plastic and so can be easily moulded to the desired shape.

An understanding of the twin capabilities of thought has led occultists to treat thoughts as entities, and to think of them as living things with shape and purpose; things that enjoy a life of their own quite independently of the mind that bore them. Additionally, it has brought them to the realization that thoughts are immensely powerful, and potentially very dangerous things.

The idea that thought is either powerful or dangerous is another concept that it is often difficult to accept — again because we persistently think of thought as being a 'no-thing' rather than as a 'some-thing'. This latter mental hurdle is, I find, best got over by even a very cursory examination of the well-attested power of thought to make us well or ill — our innate mental capacity, in other words, for internal or personal self-destruction or regeneration.

It is very generally realized these days that quite a lot of serious illness is the physiological result of psychological stress, and that we possess a compensatory mechanism that can enable us to actively retard or repel such illness. However, and insofar as we are concerned here, the very fact that we become ill in this way at all from such a cause is an indication of one of the most important capabilities of thought, and that is that it can (*whether it be deliberately initiated or not*) affect us and our environment for better or worse.

In the larger scheme of things, this means that our disregard — or ignorance — of the potential of thought has resulted in the less than perfect world we see about us. From a wholly personal standpoint, it means that all the unpleasant and fearful thoughts we think — thoughts that we are accustomed to think of as being 'harmless' and 'private' — are, in reality, neither harmless nor private, but are all the time affecting, on a subtle level, those persons at whom they are directed — including, of course, ourselves.

Appreciation of these dangerous potentialities of thought is the reason behind the occultist's preoccupation with the control of his thoughts; and this explains why so great a proportion of occult training is given over to meditation (which improves concentration) and achieving mastery of the thought processes.

In the light of the above, it should be obvious to you by now that using the technique of creative visualization to 'tamper' with reality is a project that demands considerable skill, care, and experience; and I have explained the whys and wherefores of this use of the technique at such length for two reasons. Firstly, regular practice of the techniques of meditation and visualization causes changes to occur in the levels of efficiency with which regular practitioners of those techniques think, and increases the power with which their thought is projected. Secondly, regular exercise with the technique of visualization eventually results in the practice of it — if care is not taken — becoming automatic, or not self-initiated on a conscious level.

In other words, it is quite possible to find oneself using the technique of creative visualization to affect reality while remaining quite unaware that one is doing so; and because of this, it is particularly important to learn to think, not only (literally) constructively, but also with *clarity* and *care*.

This latter is particularly important in that such mental 'actions' — despite the fact that you may be unaware of having taken them — might cause you to experience repercussions in your life. Those repercussions occur because the matrix of being is, on all its levels, constructed strictly upon the principles of polarity, or positive and negative forces in balance, and is a very *orderly* affair in which certain rules — natural laws, if you like — apply.

Those rules will operate, whether you are ignorant of them or not; and — very simply speaking — the rules of the matrix of being as they apply to the practice of creative visualization when it is used to project thought to the level where it is capable of reacting positively on its environment can be stated thus: *do as you would be done by*.

It is absolutely forbidden to use creative visualization to influence or hurt another person. Indeed, it is forbidden to use creative visualization in such a way that its use reacts in any way — detrimentally or otherwise — on any other person. This means, of course that not only must you, in the ordinary course of events, take care not to project your thoughts so as to contravene those rules, but also that — if and when you decide to use creative visualization *deliberately* — you must take extraordinary care to formulate your *intention* correctly.

The word 'intention' as it is applied here means the deliberate formulation of a proposed act, the consequences of which are planned or foreseen; and formulating intention involves mapping out, in perfect and intricate detail, any given project in all its ramifications.

The deliberate formulation of an intention closely resembles an enormous and complicated game of chess; and some appreciation of the difficulties involved can be gained by sitting down — now — and attempting to formulate an intention for something you want in such a way as to obey all the rules. You will find that the intricacies of this task — and consequently the difficulties you would experience in trying to visualize it clearly — are enormous, and in many ways quite maddening.

There are, of course, ways in which creative visualization may be used safely; and primary among these is to use intention as it was intended to be used and project change *within onself*. This is always acceptable, and (if you are going to start at all), is the proper place to begin.

The first of the exercises that follow this chapter is designed to help you master basic visualization. The second is designed to help you appreciate how force reflected out from yourself rebounds upon you from your environment. There is no time limit set on either exercise, but it is very important that you make the effort to complete both of them eventually. I emphasize this point firstly because it is very important that you understand that although the techniques of meditation and visualization may seem quite immaterial to the simple task of reading Tarot cards, *they are not*.

You will recall that in Chapter 9 we examined in some detail the 'language' of which the Tarot is constructed; and also that it was stated in that chapter that *one* of the reasons that the Tarot is constructed from a pictorial language is that such languages command universal comprehension. However, this latter is not the only reason that the Deck is constructed in this way.

There is a portion of the human mind to which the ability which we have termed 'divination' is natural; and while that 'psychic' portion of ourselves remains quite indifferent to those stimuli which attract the conscious mind, it reacts very favourably to, and is potentiated and improved by other stimuli. The symbol language of which the Tarot is constructed is one of those stimuli; meditation and visualization are two of the others — and all three are closely interrelated.

Naturally, you can use Tarot cards without ever bothering with meditation and visualization at all — or without ever expressing the smallest interest in the symbols of which the cards are constructed — but in that event, even if you are what is usually termed a 'natural psychic', you will never achieve the sort of excellence and reliability that is available to all who follow the tried and true (and very ancient) methods of psychic development that *do* involve the use of these factors.

I am particularly concerned here, too, that you complete not only the 'useful' exercises of meditation and visualization contained in this and the previous Chapter, but also that you take the trouble to complete the exercise annexed to this Chapter that is designed to illustrate the 'boomerang' behaviour of energies directed outward from the self.

All too often, the rules governing creative visualization are ignored, either because its practitioners have never experienced in any meaningful way those rules in action, or because they fail to realize — or are not taught — that the rules exist at all. This little exercise is designed both to give you that experience and to act as a timely warning, and will — hopefully — make the rules 'living' and meaningful for you.

Justice

The Daughter of the Lords of Truth; the Ruler of the Balance

Card Number:	11
Key Number:	22
Rulership:	Libra
Hebrew Letter:	Lamed
Translation:	Ox Goad (Noun) To Teach or Instruct (Verb)
Numerical Value:	12

Dignified: Legal action. Contracts. Settlement. Litigation. Divorce. Redress. Judgment. Arbitration and agreement. Treaties. Marriage sometimes, depending on surrounding cards and usually only when marriage contracts or other legal or financial documents are an integral part of the intended union.

Ill-Dignified: Separations not yet legalized or ratified by law. Legal complications. Expensive and long drawn out litigation. Inequality. Injustice and bias.

Mythological Note: The goddess Themis, goddess of abstract law, custom and equity. The goddess Maat, goddess of truth. The goddess Nemesis, the measurer of happiness and misery.

The Hanged Man

The Spirit of the Mighty Waters

Card Number: 12
Key Number: 23
Rulership: Water ▽
Hebrew Letter: Mem
Translation: Water
Numerical Value: 3

Dignified:	Willingness to adapt to changing circumstances. Flexibility of mind. Present sacrifice for future benefit. Suspension of judgement. Decisions delayed while Querent awaits the outcome of events. The sacrifice of one thing to obtain another.
Ill-Dignified:	Preoccupation with the material and the concerns of the self. A tendency to let opportunities go by for fear of losing lesser things already possessed. Preference for the status quo despite drawbacks. The devil you know, etc.
Mythological Note:	Poseidon and Neptune and all gods of the sea.

Death

The Child of the Great Transformers; the Lord of the Gate of Death

Card Number: 13
Key Number: 24
Rulership: Scorpio ♏
Hebrew Letter: Nun נ
Translation: Fish
Numerical Value: 12

Dignified:	Transformation and change as a natural result of prevailing circumstances. Physical death sometimes, but more often abrupt and complete change of circumstances, way of life, or behaviour pattern due to past actions and events.
Ill-Dignified:	Refusal to face or fear of change. Inertia. Stagnation. Forcible removal of something that should have been released voluntarily.
Mythological Note:	The gods Ares and Mars. Apep, the serpent god. Khephra the god of light in darkness. Creative force and regeneration through putrifaction.

Temperance

The Daughter of the Reconcilers; the Bringer Forth of Life

Card Number: 14
Key Number: 25
Rulership: Sagittarius
Hebrew Letter: Samech
Translation: Prop
Numerical Value: 12

Dignified: Good management. Co-ordination and co-operation. Innovation through combination. The ability to adapt to circumstance. Modification. A placid and well-balanced temperament and outlook.

Ill-Dignified: Poor judgement. A tendency to try to combine disparate activities or people, or to indulge in too many activities in too short a time. Volatility.

Mythological
Note: The goddess Diana as goddess of the chase. The god Apollo as hunter. The goddess Artemis as hunter. The god Ares as rainbow.

The Devil

The Lord of the Gates of Matter; the Child of the Forces of Time

Card Number: 15
Key Number: 26
Rulership: Capricorn ♑
Hebrew Letter: Ayin
Translation: Eye
Numerical Value: 12

Dignified: Desire for material or physical things. An indication of a propensity to collect and hoard material objects or money. Material wealth used as a tool of power. Extraordinary effort expended to ensure material success. The Querent's knowledge of his own needs and desires.

Ill-Dignified: Abuse of power and position. Comprehension of the use and value of money, possession and secular power has centred the attention on those things to the exclusion of everything else. Uncontrolled ambition. 'I want' has become 'I must have'; and this feeling includes people as well as inanimate objects.

Mythological
Note: The god Priapus, god of fruitfulness. The god Pan, god of fruitfulness. The god Bacchus representing the reproductive forces of nature. This card is emblematic of the forces of nature; the thrust of the instincts.

Instructions for the Yearly Forecast

The Yearly Forecast is intended to indicate the trends of the coming year; and each of the twelve piles of cards that make up the Spread therefore represents one complete calendar (and not Astrological) month. You should complete this Spread as follows:

1. Read and follow the instructions given in the Reader's Check List.

2. Place the Significator in a central position as shown in the diagram opposite, and then deal the cards from the top of the Deck in the pattern shown in that diagram *six cards to a pile,* i.e., the pile marked '1' on the diagram will consist of the first six cards dealt; the pile marked '2' will consist of the second six cards dealt, and so on.

3. When you have dealt the majority of the pack in the required pattern; offer the remaining cards to the Querent, and have him choose one card at random. Place that card over the Significator.

4. Discard the few remaining cards and commence reading the pile marked '1'.

    Because this Spread is intended to be a yearly forecast, the pile marked '1' will represent the current month — even if it is the last day of the current month — of the current year. The pile marked '2' will represent the coming month; the pile marked '3' the month after that, and so on.

5. The last card to be read should be that 'overlying' the Significator and forecasts the major trend of the year, i.e., if it is a Wand then the major trend for the year will be business or career matters. The success or otherwise of that trend can be adjudged from the Dignity and content of that card.

    Obviously, any difficulties or problems indicated in the Yearly Forecast can be further examined by the use of the other Spreads — preferably those that are intended to answer specific questions rather than render overall forecasts of events.

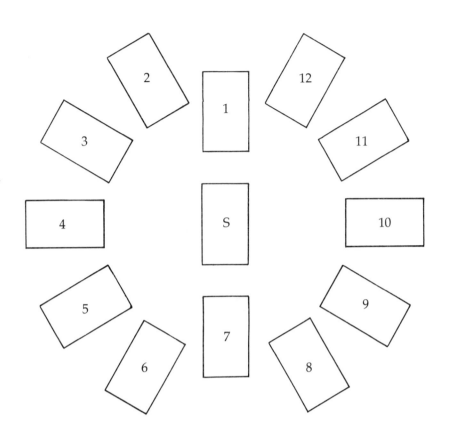

The Yearly Forecast

Visualization Exercise 1

Because visualization is such a difficult technique, it is often best to begin to try to master it with very simple 'bland' objects, rather than complex Tarot cards. Additionally, it is best to commence one 'sense' (i.e., sight, smell, etc.) at a time.

Successful visualization is best undertaken in two preliminary stages, first from one angle only, and then multi-dimensionally.

You should therefore choose an object — a matchbox, or other box, is a particularly good one to begin on — and commence to prepare to visualize one side of it only. This you should achieve with comparative ease by 'mind's eye examining' it, in the same way as you have learned to 'mind's eye examine' your cards. Take care, during this 'mind's eye' examination of your chosen object, to take note of colour, size and shape of the side of the object you are working with.

When you have finished your detailed inspection, close your eyes, and draw up a memory picture of the object as you last saw it. Thereafter, and when you have managed to visualize one side of your object as well as you possibly can, you may begin to add its other sides, one at a time and in the same way, so that you begin to see it — in your mind — dimensionally as you would in reality.

At that point, the trick is to mentally lift the box until it is hanging — in free fall as it were — in mid-air; and then mentally *turn it*, so that you see its angles changing. This is, of course, the mental equivalent of turning an object over in your hands; and it is very difficult indeed.

As the last of this series of 'one sense only' exercises — and only when you have satisfactorily completed all the others — you should attempt to visualize the box *from inside*.

It is going to take you quite some time to arrive at this level of proficiency; but while you are working on it, you can complete the other sensory visualization exercises, which are much easier, and much more fun. This means that various objects must be found on which to practise the development of the mental 'taste', 'touch', 'hear' and 'smell' senses.

Oranges make particularly good objects in this regard, because they have a strong, sharp smell, a very memorable taste and texture, and make a very good but rather subtle thud when they are dropped on a hard surface. Velvet is another good bet — and so is hessian; because, of course, they have a very distinctive feel to them. Additionally, one's hands make a noise moving across these fabrics; and most fabrics do generally have some smell attached to them, albeit a very subtle one.

There are innumerable other objects that can be used to heighten your imaginative senses. Coal, and steel cutlery; leaves and flowers both alive and dead; stones and water, both warm and cold; are all good things on which to sensitize the mental senses — and practically everything can be made to make a noise or to smell — even if only at second hand. You can smell copper, for instance, if you hold a copper coin in your hand for a few minutes or so — not on the coin, but on your skin.

There is only one thing of which you must beware when practising visualization in the ways outlined above; but it is an extremely important thing. After you have practised visualization intensively and over an extended period, you will find that it is possible to visualize objects with your eyes open; and moreover, to visualize them so well that those objects will appear to be hanging — quite objectively and superimposed on what is actually real — in the air before you.

This is a very good trick — and highly desirable in some circumstances — but only when it is achieved deliberately. Unfortunately, the first intimation that one is able to do this is quite likely to be the sudden, unexpected, and very disconcerting appearance of one of the objects of one's visualization practice, unwanted, uncalled for, but apparently nevertheless there. This can be — and often is — an object that one has practised with weeks beforehand, and it can be very, very difficult to get rid of. Got rid of, however, it must be, *immediately and whenever it occurs* — and the best way to do this is to fight fire with fire and visualize your unwanted visitor gone.

Visualization Exercise 2

1. Settle yourself into a comfortable position for meditation as usual, and then read the remainder of this exercise through carefully. When you are sure you are ready to begin, you should commence as usual.

2. When you are well settled, with your eyes closed, visualize just above your head a circle of pulsing white light.

3. When you have constructed the circle of light above your head, and when it is quite stable in your imagination, imagine that it is spilling over to form a second circle of white pulsing light at your throat. See the second circle joined to the first by a channel of light.

4. Having stabilized these two circles, construct a third circle in your solar plexus in the same way; and then a further one over your genitals, and yet another at the soles of your feet. Remember that each circle spills over from the one before it, and that all the circles are attached to each other by channels of light.

5. Having stabilized all five circles, you should be conscious of a pleasant rhythmic sensation throughout your body, and will be ready to commence the next stage of the exercise. This consists of surrounding yourself, from head to toe, with an 'egg' of white light.

6. Having stabilized all five circles and your 'egg', turn your attention to the circle above your head, and set it *spinning*.

7. When your topmost circle is spinning nicely, visualize it again spilling over, but this time as a flood *down* your left side *round* under your feet, and *up* your right side, working within your 'egg'. When it joins the circle over your head again, recommence the entire process, and keep it up for five or six turns. This should create a prickling sensation in your extremities, so if you experience this sensation don't worry about it

8. When you have completed your 'turns about' you should cease the circulation, and then start putting out 'fingers' of the light energy you have pulled in *outwards* to the walls of your room. **Make sure they stop at the walls of your room. Do not direct them at any other person. Do not put out too many in quick succession.**

9. Watch the lines carefully. You will see that they 'bounce' from the objects at which you direct them and return to you; and moreover, that the energy you receive is far greater than that you put out.

10. Record the results of this exercise and *remember* them.

It may take you a number of tries to get this exercise right, but it is worth persevering with it, for it can be used to replenish your energy and protect you from 'psychic dirt' as well as serving as an illustration of the behaviour of force.

12.

Dimensions

By now you should be aware that the faculty of clairvoyance is not some rare and magical 'gift' that is possessed by a few 'special' individuals, but a normally occurring human quality that is innate and capable of development in everyone.

The exercise of this faculty depends solely upon the ability of the would-be practitioner to shift the gears of his consciousness from one level — the ordinary sensory level he utilizes every day — to another, and very different one. That ability can be induced and perfected by practice.

Divinatory tools are designed to facilitate awareness-shift by focusing concentration in a predetermined direction and stimulating the unconscious into action. They will never induce deep, maximum shift unless they are used for *meditation** (where, as you will recall, perception shift is achieved by excluding external stimuli and turning consciousness in upon itself) rather than for simple divination; but anyone at all can induce some *degree* of perception change in himself — either by divination or meditation — if he is prepared to practise with the divinatory tool of his choice long enough, hard enough, and seriously enough.

Once achieved, the effects of awareness-shift (particularly deep awareness-shift) are very interesting indeed, because they cause reality to be perceived in a way that is fundamentally different from the norm. Obviously, these effects are less disconcerting if you are prepared for them.

When in a deeply altered state of consciousness, clairvoyants and mystics alike experience:

---

* All formally constructed divinatory tools may be used for meditation. Astrological Sigils are particularly useful subjects for this purpose, as are the I-Ching characters — but only if they are remembered and visualized correctly. An incorrectly visualized meditation subject will — obviously — produce incorrect and misleading results.

1. Altered perception of time;
2. Altered perception of the qualities we term good and evil; and
3. Altered perception of what is most important about a person, event or thing.

Of these three factors, the last is the most important, and is the causal factor behind the other two.

Altered perception factor 3 occurs because in reality as it is perceived clairvoyantly, the unity and wholeness of all things — and the interconnecting network of relationships that exists between all things — is immediately apparent.

If the state of his consciousness is sufficiently altered away from the norm, the clairvoyant experiences this unity directly, feels himself to be part of the whole he perceives, and is acutely aware of all the other units making up the whole in a very familiar and personal way. At the same time, he becomes aware of a directing and purposeful intelligence that *is* the whole — an intelligence to which he has access because he is a minute and functioning part of it.

As a direct result of altered perception, the clairvoyant finds — primarily — that he has access to knowledge that he would not ordinarily have, and thus knows things that he would not — and could not — ordinarily know. Additionally, and in the light of the manifest unity about and within him, he begins to disregard those qualities of singularity, individuality or uniqueness that are highly prized characteristics in reality as it is normally perceived, as being of no consequence; his attention focuses instead on the *relationship to the whole* of any person, event or thing.

Because of this latter drastic alteration in his priorities, the clairvoyant's perception of good and evil also undergoes a change, to the extent that he sees nothing as being good or evil *per se*, but only as being *in existence*, an essential and fundamental part of the entire tapestry of being.

Usually, this perception of good and evil differs enormously from his perception of those same factors in the sensory reality he normally inhabits, partly because in that reality the focus of his attention is narrower, and his ability to judge consequences realistically is limited by self-awareness and social mores, and in particular by *time*, which in the sensory reality adds a factor X quality to the future.

Time, however, is not a factor which must be taken into account in the clairvoyant reality, where — and due to the same altered perception factor, the clairvoyant experiences a condition of timelessness.

Events in the clairvoyant reality do not *happen*; they simultaneously *are, were* and *will be*. Thus time itself loses its familiar linear quality, and becomes instead something that might best be described as the 'Eternal Now'. Indeed, time at this awareness level can be seen to be completely illusionary, since past, present and future are equally and permanently — and quite manifestly — in existence at once.

It is this time factor, allied with a realization of the facts of existence, that precludes moral judgement by the usual standards in the clairvoyant reality.

All the effects experienced in the clairvoyant reality are diametrically opposed to the effects of the reality we experience every day. However, those facts cannot be dismissed as fantasy or simply ignored altogether, because they constitute a human experience common to all men — regardless of race or creed — who manage to achieve some degree of freedom from the shackles of the level of consciousness we term 'normal'; and so they must fit somewhere into the overall scheme of things.

To appreciate why these effects occur; and how the apparently opposing facts of the clairvoyant and material realities may be satisfactorily reconciled, we must again examine our theories about 'reality', and, more particularly, the way in which we developed those theories in the first place.

As you will recall from Chapter 11 of this book, the level of being that we think of as 'reality' is only one of several levels that together form a matrix of being that constitutes a complete whole. The material, or physical level is the densest of those levels of being, and we are equipped with five physical senses with which to deal with it — sight, hearing, taste, touch and smell. On the basis of information collected by those physical senses, we believe that objects separated by time and space are individual and separate; that events can be good or evil depending upon their consequences, and that such consequences will be revealed by time, an abstract, wholly linear condition that moves in one direction only and can be used only once.

These conclusions are, of course, absolutely valid; but they are valid only on the physical level, or the level upon which the physical senses are designed to act as information gathering devices. When the physical senses are deliberately shut down, however, or when the impact of their input is severely restricted as it is in meditation, we experience the effects of a reality where nothing is separate from anything else and where time is fluid. Moreover, the effects of that 'reality' cause us to react to events and individuals differently, so that we disregard human qualities and human social mores that would — usually — be very important to us.

That 'new' reality often appears to be quite separate, a sort of parallel universe; something that is apart from 'our' reality, and in many ways alien to it; but *it is not*. It is simply an integral, but more subtle part of the 'reality' we experience every day — and we are able to appreciate it via human sensory equipment that is designed to operate on less dense levels of the matrix of being; sensory equipment whose subtle impact is usually 'masked' or 'drowned out' by the immense input and unceasing clamour of our more ordinary physio-sensory input.

When we meditate, in fact, we 'go through' material 'reality' and 'come out' on the level that is directly behind and a part of it — a level that is accessible to us only when we are in a state of consciousness that is 'sympathetic' to it; and the facts of which are equally as valid as those of the physical reality. The clairvoyant reality can therefore be said to represent another way of looking at and evaluating our environment — a way that is just as efficient as the one we usually utilize, and which was intended to be used in conjunction with it — and the material and clairvoyant 'realities' should be regarded as two facets (but not the *only* two facets) of a complete environmental whole, both of which we are adequately equipped to deal with, but not (for the present in any event) simultaneously.

Louisa Rhinehart — a specialist in parapsychological research and thus a woman with considerable (albeit mostly second-hand) experience of the clairvoyant reality — once stated in a lecture:

> The facts of mental ability already discovered in parapsychology no more fit the current idea of a space/time world than such a fact that ships disappear bottom first over the horizon fits the model of a flat earth. The contradiction in the latter case called for a new and revolutionary idea; this one in parapsychology does too.

This is a concise statement of fact; for, at present, it is our preconceptions about 'reality', and our inability to think less myopically and be less parochial about 'reality' that is the major stumbling block to our achieving a more realistic understanding of what 'reality' really is.

Unless you meditate regularly, of course, none of the effects of the clairvoyant reality will ever trouble you at all, for the light altered state that accompanies divination merely brushes the edges of this 'other world'; but in the meantime the explanation of the facts of that reality set out above will at least go some way toward explaining some of the phenomena of divination — for divination is naturally subject to the rules of the clairvoyant rather than the sensory reality.

These rules, of course, account for the difficulties most clairvoyants experience with the time factor (that question 'Yes, but *when?*' is the bane of nearly all of us), and those occasions when we appear to be capable of reading only the past.* They also account for those readings that simply will not concentrate on the area the Querent is intent they should — namely himself — but persist in straying off into seemingly unrelated areas, turning up odd and apparently useless facts as they go.

I would point out at this juncture, however, that it is unwise to attempt to educate your Querents on the facts of the clairvoyant reality every time one of these problems raises its ugly head; because if you do you will find yourself in difficulty. Your Querent has, of course, the same sensory equipment that you have yourself — and he is just as capable of learning to use it — but he will not readily believe it if you tell him so; and, moreover, he may not be *ready* to learn to use it, nor even to acknowledge that he has it. Most clairvoyants find it quite easy to reconcile the two opposing viewpoints presented by the clairvoyant

---

* There are many good accounts of difficulties of this kind in the book *William King's Profession* by Charles Drage. Mr King was a psychometrist — a species of clairvoyant particularly vulnerable to this problem.

and sensory realities to their own satisfaction, and they are not unduly disturbed by it, *because they have had the benefit of personal experience, and possess the mental capability of accepting that experience.* The average Querent, however, has had no such experience, and so has no way of appreciating or relating to yours. Additionally, he is probably very content with his own, more conventional version of reality, and might not want that safe and comfortable vision upset. Indeed, he is much more likely to (mentally, at least) accuse you of 'making excuses' for your own 'shortcomings', and dismiss your explanations as one of the 'peculiarities' that are well-known to afflict all 'psychics' than to express any interest in your discourse whatsoever. Sadly, therefore, having the facts of two facets of reality at your fingertips is not going to make your reading life any easier; and your experiences in the clairvoyant reality are going to be yours and yours alone — unshared because unshareable — until you find another person who has had a similar personal experience.

Two Spreads are included at the end of this Chapter, and both are designed to help you deal with the problem of timing your predictions more accurately. You should complete both of them immediately you have dealt with the divinatory meanings and completed your fantasy plays in the usual way.

The Tower

The Lord of the Hosts of the Mighty

Card Number:	16
Key Number:	27
Rulership:	Mars ♂
Hebrew Letter:	Peh ב
Translation:	Mouth
Numerical Value:	9

Dignified: Change, conflict and disruption. The overthrow of an existing way of life. Change of job or residence, sometimes simultaneously. Actions which have unexpected and widespread repercussions.

Ill-Dignified: Unexpected and drastic change in circumstances. Circumstances which rob the individual of freedom of expression. Bankruptcy or imprisonment sometimes, but more usually the 'imprisonment' of the individual in a set of circumstances that he cannot, for the moment, alter.

Mythological Note: The god Horus — as god of strength. The god Mentu, god of war. The god Ares, god of war. The god Mars as god of war. The god Odin, as god of war. All warrior gods.

The Star

The Daughter of the Firmament; the Dweller between the Waters

Card Number: 17
Key Number: 28
Rulership: Aquarius ♒
Hebrew Letter: Tzaddi צ
Translation: Fish Hook
Numerical Value: 12

Dignified: Hope. Inspiration. A widening of horizons mental and physical. Influence over others. Confidence and vigour.

Ill-Dignified: Stubbornness. Rigidity of mind and outlook. Inability or unwillingness to adapt to changing circumstances or accept the opportunities that changing circumstances bring. Self-doubt and lack of trust in others.

Mythological
Note: The goddess Juno, the genius of womanhood. The goddess Athena as patron of useful and elegant arts. Ganymede as cup-bearer to the gods.

The Moon

The Ruler of the Flux and Reflux; The Child of the Sons of the Mighty

Card Number:	18
Key Number:	29
Rulership:	Pisces ♓
Hebrew Letter:	Qoph ק
Translation:	The Back of the Head
Numerical Value:	12

Dignified: Imagination. Intuition. Dreams. Psychism and psychic work sometimes. Often signifies work in the entertainment industry, particularly acting or fiction writing.

Ill-Dignified: Deception. Illusion. An inability to deal well with reality and a consequent escape into daydreams. An inability to distinguish truth from illusion sometimes. An inability to tell the truth, often.

Mythological Note: The god Neptune, as god of the sea and fish. The god Poseidon as god of the sea and fish. The god Khepera as the crab. Artemis and Hecate and all moon goddesses.

The Sun

The Lord of the Fire of the World

Card Number: 19
Key Number: 30
Rulership: The Sun ☉
Hebrew Letter: Resh ר
Translation: The Head
Numerical Value: 9

Dignified: Material happiness. Good health. An abundance of energy. Acclaim, approval, reward. Academic achievement, particularly scientific achievement. New inventors or inventions.

Ill-Dignified: Failure. Broken engagements and contracts. Troubled marriages and partnerships. Misjudgement and failure. Fantasies of success. Hypersensitivity. Hyperactivity. Autism and learning disability sometimes. Allergies, sometimes.

Mythological
Note: The gods Ra, Helios, Apollo and all gods of the solar disc. All deities representing the conscious mind.

Judgement

The Spirit of the Primal Fire

Card Number: 20
Key Number: 31
Rulership: Fire △
Hebrew Letter: Shin
Translation: Tooth
Numerical Value: 3

Dignified: Awakening. Renewal. Joy in accomplishment. Pleasure in achievement. Renewed health and vitality. Sometimes indicates the existence of decisions which must be made and which will change the life pattern for the better.

Ill-Dignified: Loss, guilt, fear of change. Fear of death sometimes. Possible ill health. Refusal to make decisions which must be made, causing delay in events.*

Mythological
Note: Agni, god of fire. Hades, god of the fiery underworld. Pluto, god of the underworld. Vulcan, god of the underworld. Tarpesheth, god of force. All these deities have to do with the internal crucible of fire wherein one state of being is transformed into another.

* If surrounding cards seem to be moving very slowly, it ought to be pointed out to the Querent that the circumstances of his life will not change until he brings himself to make the necessary decisions.

The World

The Great One of the Night of Time

Card Number:	21
Key Number:	32
Rulership:	Saturn ♄
Hebrew Letter:	Tau ת
Translation:	Cross
Numerical Value:	9

Dignified: Completion. Success. Fulfillment. A culmination of events. The end of a personal cycle, project or series of events.

Ill-Dignified: An indication that events have not yet come to a conclusion, but are nearing completion, or that a project or set of circumstances is not yet concluded despite appearances to the contrary. Fear of change sometimes.

Mythological Note: The god Pan as the sum total of all intelligences. The goddess Gaea as personification of the earth. The god Vidar representing the imperishable nature of things. The god Saturn as god of earth and agriculture. The god Sebek representing the densest form of matter. All deities representing the completed marriage of form and force.

'Yes or No, and If So, When?'
—A Reliable 'Timing' Spread

Because of the difficulty in prognosticating the timing of any given event accurately, it is always as well to include this particular Spread in your working repertoire. It is designed to provide a clear answer as to time *in response to a clearly formulated question* — a question that demands (a) the reply, 'yes' or 'no', and (b) an indication as to when the subject of the question will take place.

The Spread is a very simple one, but is nevertheless accurate. It can be used not only to obtain an answer to a given question, but also to expand upon the circumstances surrounding the question; and it depends upon the appearance, (or not, as the case may be) of any one or more of the four Aces.

You should commence (when you have shuffled and otherwise prepared the Deck) as follows:

1. Formulate the question clearly, being sure to ask 'Will I' and 'When' as part of the formulation.
2. Count off, from the top of the Deck and *face up*, one card at a time. When you have counted off thirteen cards *and if no Ace has appeared* square the pile you have made neatly, and commence to make another pile. If, however, an Ace appears *before* you reach card number 13, *stop that pile there*, and move on to the next one.
3. Complete a second pile exactly like the first, stopping only when you have either turned up an Ace or reached card number 13.
4. Complete a third pile — again stopping only when you have turned up an Ace or reached card number 13.
5. Discard all the cards that are not in one of the three piles.

Reading the results of this Spread is very easy — at least in the first instance, as the example over shows:

Pile 3   Pile 2   Pile 1

Here as you can see, we have two Aces in positions 2 and 3. One of them — the card in position 3 — is Dignified, which means that the answer to the question is 'yes'.

The positioning of the other two cards — card number 1 and card number 2, reveals that (a) the question is not yet decided (card number 1), which basically means that the Querent has not made up his mind about this situation as yet; and (b) that by *late Summer* (card number 2) the Querent *will* have made up his mind, but that the situation will *not move* until early spring (card number 3).

You may now, if you wish, read card number 1 as the reason that the Querent is hesitant; read *all* the cards in Pile 2 to ascertain why the matter is not moving at that time; and then read *all* the cards in Pile 3 to probe the events surrounding the situation when eventually it does occur.

Should you obtain 3 Aces in this spread, all Ill-Dignified, then the question is a categorial 'no', at which point you can commence to read all three piles to ascertain why not.

Should you obtain no Aces at all, then you can again read all three piles to ascertain why the question is undecided.

Whatever happens, however, you will receive a definite answer to a definite question — and a time frame to put it in.

Instructions for the Daily Spread

The Daily Spread is intended to forecast the events of a single day — and, of course, the possible outcome of any project that is under consideration on that day.

You should first commence this Spread by looking up the card that will represent the *month* in the Key to the Daily Spread on page 174. You will note that these cards are allotted to Astrological rather than calendar months. When you have found the card that will represent the month, you should lay it, Dignified, on the left of your table; and then turn your attention to finding the card for the *day*. That card too is listed in the Key to the Daily Spread, and when you have found it, it should be placed, Dignified, opposite the card of the month, on the right of your table. Take care to leave sufficient room between these two cards to lay out the rest of the Spread.

You should then follow the Reader's Check List as to shuffling, etc., and then lay out the cards in the pattern shown on page 174.

Cards 11 through 13 represent the occurrences leading up to the day in question. They should be read bottom to top, i.e., commencing with card 13 and ending with card 11.

Cards 1 through 3 on the diagram will represent the occurrences of the morning of the day in question. These three cards should be read from left to right; i.e., commencing from Card number 1.

Cards 5 through 7 on the diagram will represent the occurrences of the afternoon of the day in question; but should be read from right to left, i.e., commencing with card 7 and ending with card 5.

Cards 8 through 10 represent the evening of the day, and should be read top to bottom, i.e., commencing with card 8 and ending with card 10.

Card 4 is both the outcome of any special project that might be under consideration and the 'tone' card, i.e., card 4 will show what sort of day it will be generally. This card, must of course, be read on its own merits and according to Dignity — and it is important in this regard to realize that an Ill-Dignified card in this position will not necessarily mean that any given project will turn out badly, or that it will generally be a rotten day; for sometimes cards are better aspected when they *are* Ill-Dignified.

This Spread is particularly useful for answering specific questions about settled future events — like parties, for instance, or job interviews. It is *not* particularly useful as a daily device to be used everyday before leaving the house, and it should *not* be used in that way.

Card of the Month

Card of the Day

8

9

10

1   2   3   4   5   6   7

11

12

13

The Daily Spread

Key to the Daily Spread

Cards used to represent the Month:
ARIES — The Emperor
TAURUS — The Pope
GEMINI — The Lovers
CANCER — The Chariot
LEO — Strength
VIRGO — The Hermit
LIBRA — Justice
SCORPIO — Death
SAGITTARIUS — Temperance
CAPRICORN — The Devil
AQUARIUS — The Star
PISCES — The Moon

Cards used to represent the Day:
SUNDAY — The Sun
MONDAY — The High Priestess
                    (The Papess)
TUESDAY — The Tower
WEDNESDAY — The Magician
THURSDAY — The Wheel
FRIDAY — The Empress
SATURDAY — The World

Part Two:
The Tarot and the Tree

13.

New Horizons

If you have completed the work demanded by the previous chapters of this book properly, you will by now have absorbed enough information to make you — with practice — a competent Tarot reader. In addition, you will have come to some understanding of what you are doing, and how you are doing it; and you will have mastered as well one or two of the more basic techniques of general occult practice. This means that you have basically achieved what you set out to do when you first commenced working with this book, and now have the choice of continuing on to more difficult, more broadly based, and more rewarding work, or not, as the case may be. In this regard, it is important to understand that while Part One of this book dealt with the Tarot primarily as a divinatory tool, and presented it as a system, whole, rounded and complete unto itself, the Deck does not exist in a void; divination is not its sole, or even its primary purpose, and although it is a system complete unto itself, it is also part of a complex structure of interlocking knowledge in which many other occult arts and sciences have a place. That system is the Western Esoteric Tradition, and even if your interest in the Tarot rests purely upon its divinatory capacities, it is not a tradition that you can afford to ignore.

The body of knowledge that makes up the Western Esoteric Tradition is an enormous one, and most of it is quite beyond the scope of this book; but the cornerstone of it is a glyph called **Otz Chiim**, an understanding of which provides the key to all the rest. Consequently we shall be concentrating on that glyph and its all important Tarot attributions from now on.

Like all esoteric tools, Otz Chiim must first be studied theoretically, and then used practically; and — again like all esoteric tools — it is really the practical part of the work that is the most important part. Because of this, the remaining section of this book, like the section that preceded it, is made up of chapters, which consist of simple statements of theory; and exercises, which constitute practical work.

Insofar as the chapter material itself is concerned, it is important that you understand from the outset that you may not understand the material contained therein on your first, or even your sixth reading of it. This does not mean that you have grown particularly obtuse, or that I have grown particularly obscure. It is simply that the material itself is not such as to readily lend itself to logical comprehension.

The material will, however, crystallize into logical form *if it is approached correctly*, by way of the exercises provided.

These exercises fall into two categories: those that will prove familiar to you, and those that will not. The familiar exercises consist primarily of Reading Exercises, the only difference between those exercises and the ones you have completed hitherto being that the Spreads you will now be called upon to deal with are much larger and more complex than those to which you are accustomed. Obviously, it is to your advantage to take the trouble to complete these exercises; for while it is not the primary object of Part Two of this book to improve your prowess as a fortune-teller, it is not its object to lead you to neglect that portion of your development either. A good many occultists affect to despise the divinatory arts; but it is my belief that that attitude is both stupid and short-sighted. The act of divination exercises a faculty which is necessary to the successful practice of occultism, and thus (if justification is needed) can be said to justify itself.

Those exercises which will prove unfamiliar to you are not easy, and will demand that you exercise considerable ingenuity if you are to complete them successfully. Additionally, some of the exercises demand that you gather together various pieces of material or equipment, and this might prove troublesome to you. Obviously, it is in your own best interests to complete these exercises also, but I cannot stand over you and make sure that you complete them properly, or even at all. I can, however, assure you that if you complete them improperly you will get poor results, and that if you do not complete them at all then you will never understand the chapter material, and will be wasting your time reading it in the first place.

Insofar as a schedule of work is concerned, this should be very much the mixture as before, save that your daily work will now consist of meditation exercises, or the production of some kind of tool, rather than the simple by-rote memorization of Tarot card meanings.

Because some of the exercises are so complicated, and because some of them demand that you gather together various articles with which to work, it is advisable to read the exercises concerned at least two or three days before you envisage commencing work, so that you may have those articles ready to hand when you need them.

If you commenced work on this book as a group, then ideally you should continue to work as a group, both for the reasons given earlier in this book (which are even more valid now), and because in this way the workload can be shared, and the work itself discussed, by which means it can often be clarified.

As far as group work is concerned, however, while it is very desirable that you should continue to the end of this book — and even beyond it — as a study group, it is not desirable that you should retain any group member who wishes to leave at this point simply because you want to 'make up your numbers'. If you do retain anyone who wishes to leave — either now, or in the future — you will find that your little group will disintegrate very quickly and probably acrimoniously, and that would be a pity and a nuisance for the people who really do want to continue.

Because of the nature of the exercises, you may find that you begin to 'run over time'; that is, to exceed the time limit of one and one half hours that was set for the completion of each chapter earlier in this book. In this regard, I would ask you to remember that while it is perfectly acceptable to 'run over' for, say an hour — particularly in view of the increased volume of work that is being demanded of you — it is not at all advisable to 'run over' for three hours; and certainly three o'clock in the morning should not find you still doggedly puzzling (or doggedly arguing) over the exercises or the results of the exercises.

Finally, I would urge you to read both the chapters and exercises in this section of the book very carefully, and while you should not worry if you do not immediately understand the chapter material, you *should* make sure that you perfectly understand all the instructions for the exercises before you commence them. This is not because something dire will happen to you if you make a mistake, because it will not; but only because the exercises have been specially written or chosen to obtain the very best results for you — which they will not if you fail to follow the instructions to the letter.

14.

The Sephiroth

Although the Western Tradition is rather a portmanteau affair, with roots in the lore of many different countries, it has as its base a Hebrew philosophy — the **Qabalah**.*

The Qabalah (the word means; 'from mouth to ear', indicating that the tradition was once an oral one) is a fascinating and apparently paradoxical system that can be studied — more or less *ad infinitum* — on a multitude of different levels and from innumerable perspectives. The system is a practical and logical one — and it is beyond all logic and practicality. It is ancient beyond imagining — and it is as modern as tomorrow. It is monotheistic — and it is pantheonistic. It is Hebrew — and it is Christian.

It is all and none of these things.

Indeed, perhaps the only thing that can be said of the Qabalah with any certainty at all is that the study of it renders man, his universe and his Creator marginally more comprehensible; and so it is — logically — *everyman's* property to do with and think of as he pleases.**

On a more mundane level — but more importantly from our point of view at the moment — the Qabalah is the key and gateway to the occult, and is closely associated with the Tarot.

The primary glyph or mandala of the Qabalah — and so of the Western Tradition also — is the **Tree of Life**, which is the 'roadmap', if you like, of the larger system in which the Tarot plays such a fundamental part. The Tree of

---

* Spelling of Hebrew words varies considerably from book to book, depending upon the system of transliteration used. The meaning, of course, remains the same.
** And therein lies the secret of the system's perfection and universal appeal — for every man who does use it comes eventually to the same conclusion: that all is One, and that the schisms and contradictions that appear inherent in the system — and are so mirrored in life itself — are an illusion and a nonsense.

Life illustrates, symbolically, a process of manifestation, or *force* precipitating into *form*.*

'Force' and 'form' are in reality *one and the same thing*; for form is constructed of organized force. Force in organization undergoes an increase in complexity and density on descending the Tree, and that increase takes place in four orderly and clearly defined stages which we will examine in more detail in a later chapter. For the time being, however, the concept to grasp here is that force organized into form on the densest and most material of these four stages constitutes the universe we live in and everything in it.

Form structures — and that includes, of course, the universe and the bodies we presently inhabit — maintain themselves for a certain length of time before breaking up and releasing the force in organization of which they are constructed back into the system to be recycled; for only the *shape* which is the visible manifestation of the eternal force is infinite; while the life force which inhabits the temporary form is eternal.**

As you will see from the diagram on page 182 the construction of the Tree of Life is comparatively simple. It is formed of ten circles linked by twenty-two lines so as to make a pattern.

The circles are called **Sephiroth**‡ or Major Paths of Wisdom, and represent established forms of existence (form concepts). The lines are called the Minor Paths of Wisdom and represent established forms of consciousness (force concepts).

Above the lines and circles, in a pattern resembling a rainbow, you will see that there are three separate arc-shaped lines marked 'Ain', 'Ain Soph' and 'Ain Soph Aur'.

Above them again — and unmarked on the diagram for reasons that will become immediately obvious — is The Unmanifest.

---

* The word 'force' in this context is considered to imply an infinite, purposefully directed creative energy; while the word 'form' implies a finite vehicle — a limiting, disciplining factor that provides the force energy with a means of expression and an environment for optimum growth and development.

** This latter is a very imporant concept, and one that is fundamental to the philosophy as a whole. On a very mundane level indeed, it means that when *you* die, you do not cease to be — at least not entirely — for the human body replicates exactly the form/force formula described above; and breaks up and recycles in exactly the same way. The very complex concept of man and his various 'sheathes' or bodies is best described in *The Cosmic Doctrine* by Dion Fortune, but simply speaking, the physical you — the body you presently inhabit — is the most temporary of all your bodies, and will eventually cease to exist in its present form. That portion of yourself that constitutes your personality is marginally more durable, but that too eventually 'dies' — and it is this that constitutes the 'second death' that is sometimes referred to in occult literature. The essential you, however, or that which is called 'the individuality' and of which the more temporary personality is an (often deviated) expression, is very enduring indeed, and lasts for an entire Cosmic Cycle.

‡ Singular Sephira, meaning Emanation(s).

The Unmanifest is the root and source of the Tree in that it is the place from which all manifestation originally proceeds, but it is unimaginable and inexplicable to us, because it is both infinite and devoid of form as we know it, and is thus beyond the scope of minds shaped — as ours are — by the limitations of a manifest and finite reality.

Ain, Ain Soph and Ain Soph Aur, or 'nothingness' 'limitlessness' and 'limitless light' respectively, are jointly referred to as The Three Veils of Negative Existence. They symbolize the three ways in which force can manifest — active, passive, and equilibrized — and the process by which the first Sephira came forth from The Unmanifest into manifestation, thereafter to spill over or emanate the remaining nine Sephiroth of itself.

The top three Sephiroth, or those numbered 1 through 3 on the diagram below are called the **Supernals,** and together form a triangle called **The Supernal Triangle.**

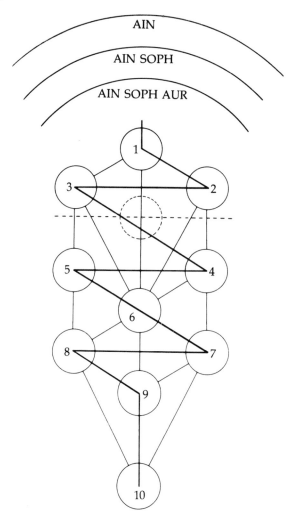

The Tree of Life

The Supernals represent ideal states; conditions that are perfect, and so (for the present, in any event) incomprehensible to us. The remaining Sephiroth, or those numbered 4 through 10 on the diagram, are called the **Inferiors**, and are considered to have fallen from the state of perfection normal to the Superiors.*

The Inferiors are separated from the Supernals by a fixed gulf. This gulf is called **The Abyss,** and its whereabouts is marked on the diagram on page 182 by a horizontal broken line which directly divides the unnumbered (and sometimes unmarked) Sephira D'aath; the position of which is indicated on the diagram by a dotted circle. The Abyss is one of three such gulfs on the Tree, the other two being the veils of **Paroketh** and **Qesheth**. The Veil of Paroketh divides the **Ethical** triangle from the **Astral** triangle (see diagram on page 184; while the Veil of Qesheth stands directly above the Sephira numbered 9. All three gulfs represent barriers to the free passage of force (and therefore consciousness) up and down the Tree.

The Sephiroth are considered to have manifested in a fixed order called the **Path of the Lightning Flash** (illustrated on the diagram on page 182 by a thick black zig-zag line), each Sephira emanating, or overflowing, from one directly above it, i.e., Sephira 2 from Sephira 1; Sephira 3 from Sephira 2 and so on until the Tree in its entirety achieves stability on the formation of Sephira 10. Each Sephira can therefore be said to have emanated from the first 'form expression' of the infinite creative force first expressed in Sephira 1, and is considered to work out a fresh facet of that original expression.

It is in this concept of 'facets of the Creator' that the Tree can be said to be pantheonistic; and this is a perfectly acceptable interpretation *so long as it is borne in mind that each facet is only a facet and nothing more.* The idea that a single facet is or ever can be the be-all and end-all is where the trouble starts — and there has been considerable trouble about this before now.

The names allotted to these Sephiroth go some way — but not very far — toward explaining the concepts behind these expression facets, and are shown on the diagram on page 184. As you will see, these names appear in large bold print transliterated from the original Hebrew, with English translations relegated to secondary status underneath. The reason for this is twofold.

Firstly, the names of the Sephiroth and the letters of which the names are constructed convey information that cannot be conveyed accurately by translation — all translations of any one language into another being by definition imperfect.

---

* You should beware here, however, of applying the words: 'supernal' and 'inferior' too literally; or misinterpreting the words: 'fallen from...(a)... state of perfection'; for we are here distinguishing 'incomprehensible' from '(semi) comprehensible' rather than 'best' from 'not so good'; the Inferiors being in no way *literally* inferior to the Superiors. Confusion may be avoided here by bearing in mind that both these words once had rather different meanings to the ones they carry today, and were allotted to the various Sephiroth some time ago.

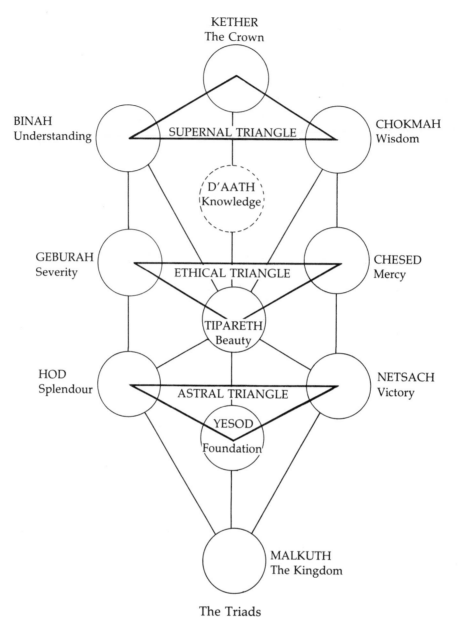

The Triads

Secondly, these words are **Words of Power,** and are therefore capable of causing changes in consciousness when pronounced correctly.

While these points may not seem to be (and almost certainly aren't) of vital importance to you at the moment, it is nevertheless still very important that you familiarize yourself with the transliterations provided *now*, rather than seeking to avoid the language problem by learning only the translations, for this is not a problem that will go away just because you decide to ignore it. It is in any event not nearly such a difficult task as it might appear to be, foreign words being frequently more memorable than familiar ones by reason of the fact that they are exotic.

Insofar as pronunciation is concerned, the main thing to remember is that Ch in Hebrew is pronounced H as in *home* rather than Ch as in *chocolate* (i.e., Chokmah is pronounced 'Hokma'). Otherwise the Hebrew words you will be concerned with look very much the way they should sound.

While all the cards of the Tarot Deck can be placed on the Tree of Life, it is the cards of the Minor Arcana that are associated with the Major Paths of Wisdom — an allocation that you will realize to be absolutely logical when you consider that both the cards of the Minor Arcana and the Sephiroth themselves represent established forms of being, or realities.

Small cards are placed according to their face value, which corresponds very conveniently to the numbering system of the Sephiroth. Thus all Aces (Ones) belong in the Sephira Kether (1); all Twos in the Sephira Chokmah (2), and so on.

Court cards present a slightly more difficult proposition. They are placed on the Tree according to the small diagram below:

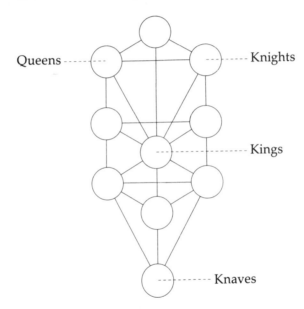

Thus, all Knights are attributed to Chokmah (2), with the Twos; all Queens are attributed to Binah (3), with the Threes: all Kings are attributed to Tipareth (6), with the Sixes; and all Knaves are attributed to Malkuth (10), with the Tens.

The four Suits of the Minor Arcana *as a whole* also have a place on the Tree. They are attributed as follows:

All **Wands** *as a Suit* are attributed to **Chokmah** with the **Knights** and the **Twos**.

All **Cups** *as a Suit* are attributed to **Binah** with the **Queens** and the **Threes**.

All **Swords** *as a Suit* are attributed to **Tipareth** with the **Kings** and the **Sixes**.

All **Pentacles** *as a Suit* are attributed to **Malkuth** with the **Knaves** and the **Tens**.

As you will recall, Elemental and other attributions were made to the four Suits of the Minor Arcana at the very beginning of this book, and it is from the Tree of Life attributions that these were culled. From information you have already absorbed, therefore, you should now begin to be able to work out for yourself some of the other Tree attributions. The Element of Fire, for instance, was attributed to the Suit of Wands. This means that the Element of Fire can also be attributed to Chokmah, the home Sephira of the Suit of Wands — as can the Yod portion of the Divine Name, which we also attributed a long time ago to the Suit of Wands. Indeed, once all the Elements have been accurately placed upon the Tree, every attribution that you earlier learned by rote can be seen to be perfectly logical. The Knave of Wands, for instance, is called Earth of Fire because he is a Wand (home Sephira Chokmah = Fire), and a Knave (home Sephira Malkuth = Earth).

In reality, therefore, only a few of the Minor Arcana cards can be related to one single Sephira, and considered to be the essence of their Suit. These cards are:

The Two and Knight of Wands
The Three and Queen of Cups
The Six and King of Swords
The Ten and Knave of Pentacles

This is because only these eight cards of the whole Deck are of the same Sephira according to Face Number (or Name) and according to their Suit. Apart from these eight cards, every other card of the Minor Arcana will take attributions from two different Sephira, i.e., the Sephira of its Face Number, and the home Sephira of its Suit.

Because the contents of this chapter are rather complex, three separate sets of exercises accompany it, all of which are designed to help you retain the new information you need to continue on to the next chapter. Two of these exercises should be completed immediately, but the third may be completed at your convenience, so long as it is, at some time in the future, assimilated and worked on.

As usual, you should first complete the exercises and at least two sets of fantasy plays; and then move on to the Spread without delay. The Spread for this chapter is called 'The Tree of Life Spread', and is designed — like the exercises and this chapter itself — simply to familiarize you with the way the Tree is constructed. You should *not*, therefore, attempt to relate any of the new information contained in this chapter to the cards as you are reading them — or even the place meanings of the Sephiroth as they appear in the Spread to the Tree of Life itself — for the very good reason that you won't be able to. Neither, incidentally, should you sit down and have a little meditate — however tempting an idea that might seem — for the time for that is not yet either. In fact — for the moment at any rate — all that is required of you is that you recognize the Tree when you see it, and that you be so aware of its salient features as to be able to actually point them out to someone in the (admittedly unlikely) contingency that they should ask you to. This means, of course, that you are faced with yet another of those difficult and boring periods the like of which have driven you mad throughout this book — a time of learning by rote without really understanding what you are doing. Unfortunately, however, the only real way to build a house — whether it be a physical house or a house of knowledge — is to put one brick on top of another and look forward to the day when you can put the roof on and throw away the plans.

Exercise 1

1. Printed below are six small diagrams of the Tree of Life. Fill in each diagram according to its heading, i.e., the diagram headed 'Elemental Attributions' should bear the names of the elements in the appropriate Sephira; and so on.

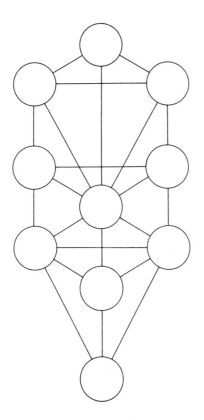

Elemental Attributions

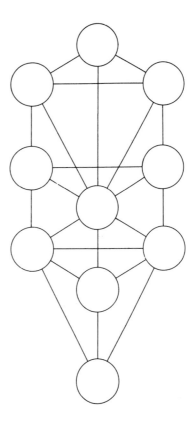

Court Card Attributions

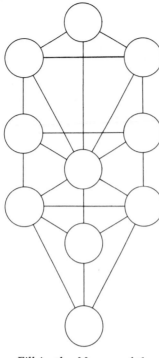

Fill in the Names of the
Sephiroth

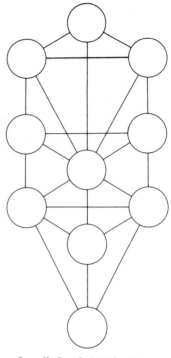

Small Card Attributions

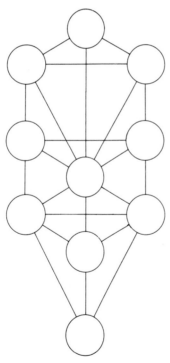

Fill in the Path of the
Lightning Flash

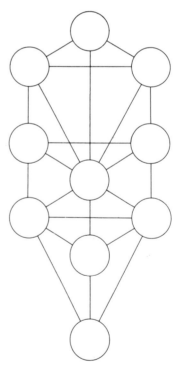

Draw Three Lines to Mark
The Three Veils of
Negative Existence

2. What does the word 'Qabalah' mean?...

3. The spelling of Hebrew words varies from book to book. Why?................
....

4. What is the primary mandala of the 'Qabalah' called?............................
....

5. There are twenty-two lines on the Tree of Life. What are they called?.........
....

6. How many Sephiroth are there?..

7. There is another name for the Sephiroth. What is it?..............................

8. What do the Major Paths of Wisdom represent?...................................

9. Ain, Ain Soph, and Ain Soph Aur can be jointly referred to as.................

10. Which three Sephiroth form the Supernal Triangle?.............................
....

11. The Inferiors are those Sephiroth numbered......through........................

12. The Inferiors are separated from the Supernals by the Abyss. There are two other gulfs like the Abyss on the Tree. What are they called?..............
....

13. There are three named Triangles on the Tree of Life. One of them is the Supernal Triangle. What are the other two called?...............................

14. The Sephiroth are considered to have manifested in a fixed order. What is that order called?...

15. To which Sephiroth is the Suit of Wands attributed?.............................

16. How many cards of the Minor Arcana can be said to be the essence of their Suit; and why?...

17. To which Sephira are all Knights attributed?......................................

18. What is the meaning of the word 'Sephira'?..

Exercise 2

Requirements:
   1.   10 plates or 10 pieces of paper.
   2.   1 pair of scissors.
   3.   1 ball of yarn or reel of sewing cotton.
   4.   1 marking pen.
   5.   28 small slips of paper.
   6.   1 roll of *Sellotape*.
   7.   1 Tarot Deck.

1. Take ten plates or cut ten pieces of paper into a round shape. These will be used to represent the Sephiroth, so although it really doesn't matter what you use, it is better if all your materials are of equal size and shape — so try not to use a mixture of dinner and cake plates, and if you are using paper, try to cut it uniformly. If you are using patterned plates, turn them over so that the white side is uppermost.

2. Place the material you are using to represent the Sephiroth on the floor in the pattern shown in the diagram on page 182. Make sure to lay out your material in the right order — i.e., following the Path of the Lightning Flash. You need not bother to indicate the position of the unnumbered Sephira at this time; but you should try to make the spaces between individual Sephira even and uniform, as they are in the diagram.

3. Mark the plates with the marking pen, 1 through 10.

4. Cut twenty-two pieces of yarn or sewing cotton into equal lengths, and reproduce the Minor Paths of Wisdom on your 'diagram'; anchoring the ends of the yarn/cotton firmly under the plates. If you are using cut paper, punch a hole through the centre of the paper with the end of your pencil, and poke the ends of the cotton through the hole, so that they are hidden underneath the paper.

5. When you have finished your model, step back and examine it carefully. Make sure that everything is in its proper place before continuing.

6. When you are quite sure that your model is the way it should be, take the twenty-eight slips of paper and divide them into seven piles, four slips to each pile.

7. On the first four slips, write the names of the four Elements, one to each slip. *Sellotape* these slips to the plates so that they correctly indicate the elemental allocations of the Tree.

8. On the next four slips, write the names of the four Suits, one to each slip. *Sellotape* these slips too to the plates, so that they correctly indicate the allocations of the four Suits *as a whole* to the Tree.

9. On the next batch of slips, write the four sections of the Divine Name, one section to each slip. *Sellotape* these slips to their corresponding Sephiroth.

10. On the next batch of slips, write the Elemental Names of the four Pages. *Sellotape* these slips to their corresponding Sephira.

11. On the next batch of slips, write the Elemental Names of the four Knights.

Sellotape these slips to their corresponding Sephira.

12. On the next batch of slips, write the Elemental Names of the four Queens. *Sellotape* these slips to their corresponding Sephira.

13. On the last batch of slips, write the Elemental Names of the four Kings. *Sellotape* these slips to their corresponding Sephira.

14. Divide the Minor Arcana from the rest of the Deck; and then divide the Small from the Court cards.

15. Lay the Small cards out on the plates so as to correctly attribute them to each Sephira. There will be four cards to each plate, and these cards should be 'fanned' so that all the cards are at least marginally visible.

16. Extract the four Knaves from the Court cards, and place them, 'fanned' on the plate representing their home Sephira. Do likewise with the four Knights, Queens and Kings.

17. When you have placed all the cards and slips on the construct, check these placings carefully against the text to make sure they are all in the right place. If you find that you have placed everything correctly, gather up your cards and proceed to the Spread *leaving your basic model, and all the slips of paper on the floor for the moment.* If you have not placed everything correctly on the construct, note and correct your mistakes before going any further.

Exercise 3

Make a permanent model like the one described in Exercise 2 of this Chapter.

To make this model you will need:
1.   10 paper plates.
2.   1 ball of yarn.
3.   1 pair of scissors.
4.   2 wire coat-hangers.
5.   1 box of paperclips or 78 clothes pegs.
6.   1 marking pen.

1. Punch four small holes in the centre of each plate, like so:

2. Sew the first plate to the hook of one of the coat-hangers, so:

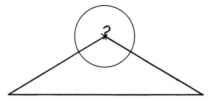

This plate will represent Kether.

3. Sew the second and third plates to the two ends of this same coat-hanger, so that your construct looks like this:

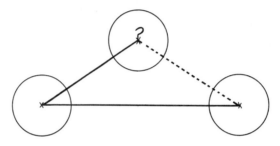

These plates will represent Chokmah and Binah.

4. Run a piece of yarn from Kether down through Chokmah, and leave a sufficient length of thread hanging to enable you to attach a plate to represent Chesed to the end of it, so that your model looks like this:

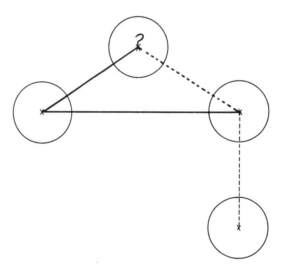

5. Continue to attach plates to the construct in the same way until you arrive at the two plates which will represent Netsach and Hod, so that your model looks like this:

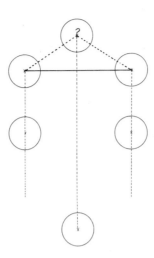

6. Attach the two plates that will represent Netsach and Hod to the second of the two coat-hangers; *invert the coat-hanger so that the hook is hanging below the plates,* and then sew the plates and the hanger to the main construct. You will now find that when you hold the construct by the topmost hook (or that 'behind Kether' so to speak) the second hanger will weight it, so that it hangs straight.

7. Attach the plate which will represent Yesod to the construct by sewing it to the second of the two coat-hangers, leaving a sufficient length of yarn to allow you to attach the plate representing Malkuth to the construct.

8. When you have attached the plate which will represent Malkuth, your model will look like this:

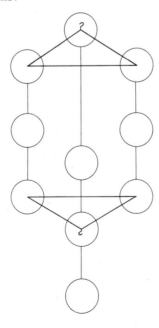

and you should now proceed to fill in the missing Minor Paths of Wisdom by cutting off lengths of yarn and sewing them to the plates.

If you hang the model by the hook of the topmost coat-hanger you will find that you have a very satisfactory mobile, on which you should write the elemental attributions and other information as it comes along. It is also a good idea, once in a while, to 'peg out' your Deck to the model — cards of the Minor Arcana to be pegged to the plates; cards of the Major Arcana to be pegged to the yarn. If you would like to, you can also make large Hebrew letters and large Astrological signs and peg those up too, for this 'Kim's Game' will help you to learn the various attributions of the Tree much faster than anything else.

Instructions for the Tree of Life Spread

1. Have the Querent shuffle and cut as usual. Do *not* look for or extract a Significator from the Deck.

2. Lay out the *entire Deck* as per the diagram for the Spread.

3. Go through the ten groups of cards thus constructed until you find the pile that contains the Significator. *Do not discard the other piles.*

4. Read the pile containing the Significator having reference to the Position Meanings listed below, i.e., if the Significator is found in pile number 3, the subject of that mini-reading will be: Sorrows and Burdens, or that which is troubling the Querent.

5. When you have read the pile containing the Significator, *read all the other piles as well, one-by-one, commencing with pile number 10.*

This Spread is obviously a very time-consuming one; but it is worthwhile in that it gives such a good overall picture of what is going on in the Querent's life — and how he feels about it. It is difficult, at first, to relate the different piles one to another — for they are, of course, all interrelated — but this is a knack that comes with practice. It is *not* wise, in the beginning, however, to turn over all the piles at once in an effort to locate the common denominator, because this is confusing.

The spread usually covers the usual six-month period.

Position Meanings
1. (Kether)   —   Inner Spiritual Quest.
2. (Chokmah) —   Personal Initiative.
3. (Binah)   —   Sorrows and Burdens.
4. (Chesed)   —   Financial Gains.
5. (Geburah)   —   Enemies and Discords.
6. (Tipareth)   —   Glory and Fame.
7. (Netsach)   —   Love.
8. (Hod)   —   Wheeling, Dealing and Communications.
9. (Yesod)   —   Mental and Physical Health.
10. (Malkuth)   —   The Home.

```
                        1
                       11
                       21
                       31
                       41
                      etc.


    3                                                   2
   13                                                  12
   23                                                  22
  etc.                                                etc.


    5                                                   4
  etc.                                                etc.




                        6
                      etc.




    8                                                   7
  etc.                                                etc.




                        9
                      etc.




                       10
                      etc.
```

The Tree of Life Spread

15.

Three Pillars

If you look at the diagram on page 198, you will see that the ten Sephiroth of the Tree of Life form three vertical pillars — **The Pillars of Manifestation**.

The pillar on the right-hand side of the Tree, or that formed by the Sephiroth Chokmah, Chesed and Netsach is called the **Pillar of Mercy**; it is usually coloured white or silver, and is considered to represent *Cosmic Force.*

The pillar on the left-hand side of the Tree, or that formed by the Sephiroth Binah, Geburah and Hod is called the **Pillar of Severity**. The Pillar of Severity is feminine and passive; it is usually coloured black, and is considered to represent *Cosmic Form.*

The Pillars of Mercy and Severity are sometimes jointly referred to as the **Pillars of Function**.

The four Sephiroth forming a straight line up the centre of the Tree (Malkuth, Yesod, Tipareth and Kether, together with the unnumbered Sephira D'aath) form the third pillar — the **Pillar of Equilibrium**

The Pillar of Equilibrium is considered to represent *Form* and *Force* in balance, and the element of *consciousness* in the cosmic equation. It is sometimes called the **Middle Pillar**, and is neither masculine nor feminine, but takes the attributes of both.*

The Three Pillars of Manifestation, like the Three Veils of Negative Existence, have reference to the three ways in which force can manifest — active (masculine); passive (feminine), and equilibrized; but unlike the Three Veils, which are an integral part of the Tree and which exist as an essential preliminary to manifestation, the Three Pillars have existence in their own right whether or not manifestation is present. They are therefore quite

---

* Consciousness is considered to be neither pure force nor pure form. Thought, for instance, has shape, but it is intangible in comparison with the much denser forms with which we are surrounded *on this plane*. Other, less dense levels, however, are capable of being moulded or changed by the impact of thought — hence (and because everything that is formed *there* eventually comes to be *here*) the occult adage: 'Thoughts are Things'; and the occultist's preoccupation with the control of his thoughts.

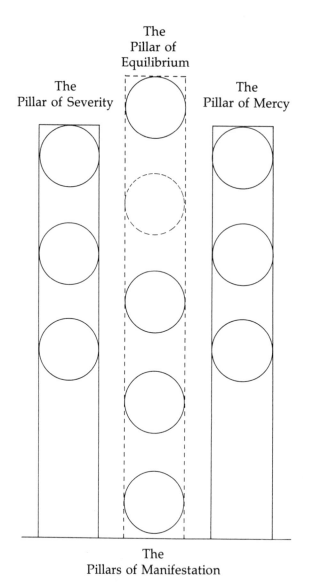

The
Pillar of
Equilibrium

The
Pillar of Severity

The
Pillar of Mercy

The
Pillars of Manifestation

separate from the Tree — or at least they may be studied, as abstracts, quite separately from it.

The principle of masculine (active) and feminine (passive) forces operating against a balance is called the **Principle of Polarity**, and is basic to Qabalistic philosophy, which teaches that all manifestation is based upon the tension created by *duality*. The Principle of Polarity is at its most obvious in the relationship of the Three Pillars, but it operates all over the Tree, establishing a complex network of polarizing relationships that exist in a state of *stress*. I emphasize the word 'stress' because it is only too easy — particularly in the case of the Three Pillars — to imagine these two forces and their balancing agent 'hanging loose' as it were, in time and space; immobile, perpetually in perfect harmony, and thus inert.

This is very far from the case. A much better analogy — again using the

Three Pillars — is the Middle Pillar as pendulum; swinging this way and that, responding to the pull exerted from one direction and then the other; preserving a balance that is *compensatory* rather than perfect, so that the whole exists in a state of tension and vibrancy. Such tension creates an environment in which change, growth and evolution all flourish — the sort of environment which could never exist in a condition of inertia, which is, by definition, one of stagnation, decay and decline.

The interlocking system of relationships on the Tree as defined by the Principle of Polarity commences of course, with the appearance of the Three Veils of Negative Existence; and so to examine it properly we must again return to the difficult concept of the Unmanifest; that unimaginable state of being that simply *is*.

The Unmanifest is a condition that might best be thought of as a state of *latent potency*, out of which develops firstly the Three Veils of Negative Existence (Ain, Ain Soph, and Ain Soph Aur), and — eventually Kether and the rest of the Tree.

In order to try and comprehend this process — the manifestation of an apparent something from an apparent nothing — one must undertake to imagine the latently potent *is* of the Unmanifest commencing to move in a circle. It does not matter, of course, that it is quite impossible to imagine any such thing *properly*, for both the *is* and the proposed movement are symbols designed to assist comprehension of the incomprehensible and nothing more — a fact that it is best to keep well to the forefront of the mind when undertaking this exercise. This first movement, or circle, is called **Ring Cosmos**.

The movement of Ring Cosmos causes a further ring — **Ring Chaos** — to appear at right angles to it, thus:

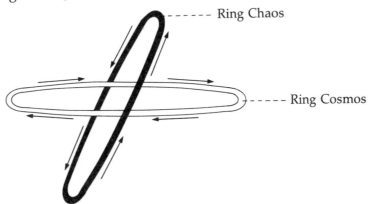

Ring Cosmos is considered to be the first manifestation of the masculine principle, while Ring Chaos is its complementary feminine counterpart. Thus, on the formation of these two rings, the duality which Qabalistic Philosophy considers to be the basis of manifestation can be considered to exist.

Ring Cosmos and Ring Chaos together form an axis at their point of connection, so that the first ring begins to rotate *transversely* against the thrust block of the second. This in turn promotes the birth of a third ring; **Ring Pass Not**.

Ring Pass Not is so called because it forms a shield around the rest. This Ring limits further development, or (as my own teacher once put it) stops prospective manifestation 'fraying at the edges', or dissipating itself. Ring Pass Not, of course, also completes the triad of forces necessary to ensure manifestation; for it *equilibrizes* the other two, thus:

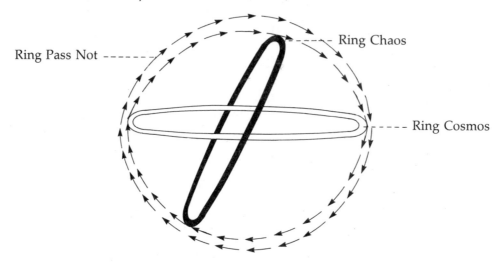

These three Rings, Cosmos, Chaos, and Pass Not, equate to Ain, Ain Soph and Ain Soph Aur respectively; and it is the transverse spin of Cosmos (Ain) which causes the appearance — or concrete manifestation — of Kether.*

The pattern so set by the three Rings 'sets the tone' as it were, for the rest of the Tree, and the Principle of Polarity that operates there is reproduced everywhere else. Thus, each Sephira polarizes vertically; horizontally; along the Path of the Lightning Flash, and *within itself*, for no Sephira is wholly masculine nor wholly feminine, despite its positioning on the Tree or its relationship to one or another of the Three Pillars. The rule of thumb to follow here is that every Sephira is masculine and positive to the one below it, and feminine and negative to the one above it; each pair of Sephiroth positioned one on each of the Pillars of Function finding equilibrium in a Sephira located on the Middle Pillar (i.e., Chokmah and Binah balance in Kether to form the Supernal Triangle; Chesed and Geburah in Tipareth to form the Ethical Triangle; and so on). The Major Paths of Wisdom, of course, polarize with the Minor Paths.

The main exercise for this Chapter is to draw the Tree of Life by following the

---

* If you find it difficult to visualize transverse spin — and most people do — I find it helps considerably to watch water disappearing down a plug hole — preferably a lot of water down a very small plug hole — because this reproduces very nicely the illusion of one ring spinning transversely (or in two directions at once), as well as the illusion of a solidifying core.

instructions on page 202. When you have completed the drawings you should then go on to fill in all the information you have received to date and, from that information, plot the numerical sequence of each card within the Tarot Deck — which sequence, incidentally, commences with The Fool and ends with the Ten of Pentacles.

When you have completed the entire exercise and the series of questions that precede it, you should go on with your fantasy plays and then complete the Spread as usual.

Exercise 1

1. What are the three Pillars together called?...................................

2. One of the three Pillars is usually coloured white or silver. What is the name of that Pillar?...................................

3. Which Sephiroth can be found upon the Pillar of Mercy?...................
....

4. What are the two outermost Pillars of the Tree sometimes jointly referred to as?...................................

5. What does the Pillar of Equilibrium represent?...........................
....

6. What is an alternative name of the Pillar of Equilibrium?...................
....

7. The principle of masculine (active) and feminine (passive) forces operating against a balance is called...................................

8. Draw a small diagram of the three rings, and label each ring:

9. Why is the Ring Pass Not so called?...................................
....

10. Which of the three Rings represents the feminine principle?...................
....

11. Which of the three Rings relate to:
    i)   Ain...................................
    ii) Ain Soph...................................
    iii) Ain Soph Aur...................................

Exercise 2
Drawing the Tree of Life

To complete this exercise, you need a ruler, a compass and a pencil.

It is very important, when drawing this glyph, to remember that all the Sephiroth are equidistant from each other. If this is borne carefully in mind, then the proportions of your Tree will be correct, whatever size you choose to draw it.

1. To begin your drawing, take a piece of paper and your ruler and pencil. Using the ruler to guide you, make five dots down the centre of your paper, 2in (5cm) apart. These five dots will be the central point of the Sephiroth Kether, D'aath, Tipareth, Yesod and Malkuth.

2. Next, take your compasses and set them against the ruler at a measure of 2in (5cm) — i.e., the point and the pencil of your compass should be 2in (5cm) apart. Using the five dots you have drawn, place the point of the compass in the centre of the Sephira Kether, and draw a small arc on each side of that Sephira (See diagram B opposite).

3. Continue this process down the Tree until you have small arcs beside every Sephira save Malkuth. At this point your diagram should look like the one marked B opposite. The points where the arcs intersect form the central points of those Sephiroth which make up the Pillars of Wisdom and Severity.

4. Reset your compasses to a measure of 1in (2.5cm) and using the central dots, and the intersection points of the arcs as your guide, draw circles to represent each Sephira.

5. With your ruler, draw in the Minor Paths of Wisdom on the Tree. These are best drawn as channels, so that you may use the space between two lines to fill in the various attributions, etc. You should copy the Minor Paths of Wisdom carefully by looking at the completed diagram D opposite.

6. Fill in all the Tree attributions you have learned to date.

Later, when you have more time, and are used to drawing the glyph of the Tree of Life, it is a good idea to buy a large sheet of paper or stiff card, and make a really good painting of the Tree that you can use more or less permanently.

Diagram A:
Make five dots with your ruler.

Diagram B:
Making arcs with a compass.

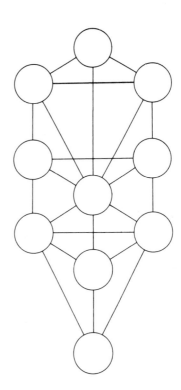

Diagram C:
Drawing circles using the dots and arcs.

Diagram D:
The completed Tree showing all the paths.

Instructions for the Sixteen Card Spread

1. Place the Significator as per the diagram opposite.

2. Dealing from the top of the Deck (and after following the instructions in the Reader's Check List), lay out the remainder of the Spread as per the diagram, 'covering' the Significator with card number 1.

3. Commence the reading with card number 1. This card signifies the Querent's primary concern and his present situation generally.

4. Cards 2 and 3 should next be read, as these cards give further depth to the primary question and also throw some light on the Querent's character and personality. This is particularly true, of course, if either or both of these cards happen to be Major Arcana cards.

5. Cards 14, 10 and 6 (which should also be read in that order) show how the Querent arrived at his present position. They are the background of the situation.

6. Card 7, 11 and 15 (which should also be read in that order) indicate the activities of other people in the situation.

7. Cards 4, 8 and 12 (read in that order) show the direction in which matters will progress, and should of course be read in the light of cards 7, 11 and 15

    This latter direction may, of course, be changed, *but only if at least two of the cards in set 7, 11 and 15, and two of the cards in set 4, 8 and 12, are Minor Arcana cards.*

    If more than one card in either set is a Major Arcana card, then the situation will progress in the direction shown whether the Querent wills it or not.

8. Cards 13, 9 and 5 (read in that order) show the possibilities for alternative action, if any.

    In this latter regard, if cards 4, 8 and 12, or cards 7, 11 and 15 consist primarily of Major Arcana cards — which means that no actual *alternative* action may be taken — cards 13, 9 and 5 will indicate how the outcome may be marginally mitigated (in case of a poorly aspected outcome) or assisted (in case of a well aspected outcome).

The Sixteen Card Spread can be difficult to work with, because in this Spread more than practically any other each card *must* be read in the light of all the others; but it is an excellent Spread to use whenever an in-depth look at a single situation is demanded.

Because the Spread is so difficult to work out, it is often best to have the

Querent ask his question aloud. It is also of assistance, sometimes, to lay the cards out *face down* on the table, rather than face up, since in this way they can be turned over and evaluated one-by-one — exactly as they are in a fantasy play. This means that you will have little chance to work out the 'story line' of the Spread in your head before you commence; but sometimes this, too, is advisable — particularly when the Querent is asking his questions aloud — since it also dispenses with the preconceptions that sometimes occur under those circumstances and when time is taken to develop the 'story line' of the Spread.

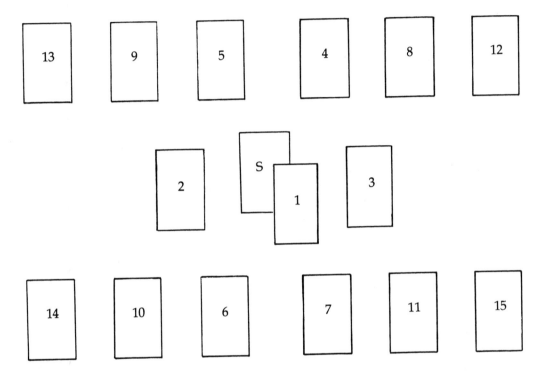

The Sixteen Card Spread

16.

Four Worlds

The Tree of Life can be divided into four sections that are usually called the **Four Worlds of the Qabalists**. This new division has the effect of isolating sections of the Tree, and labelling those sections as both stages in the manifestation of the whole, and as to *function*. The diagram opposite shows how the Tree looks when it is divided in this way.

As you will see from that diagram, Kether, the topmost Sephira, occupies the first world alone. This world is called **Atziluth**, and is the Archetypal World, or the World of the Pure Spirit.

Chokmah and Binah, sometimes called 'The Father' and 'The Mother' respectively, occupy **Briah**, the Creative World, which appears as the second world on the diagram.

Chesed, Geburah, Tipareth, Netsach, Hod and Yesod together form the third of the four worlds, **Yetzirah**, or the Formative World; and Malkuth, the sole remaining Sephira, occupies **Assiah**, or the Physical World alone.

The underlying concept of the Four Worlds is as follows:

The World of Atziluth is considered to be the highest level of manifest existence, and is thus known as the Archetypal World for it contains the first pattern of that which is to be.

The World of Briah is also considered to be of a spiritual nature, and is the most important to us, because this is the level upon which most of the work must be done. Briah represents a level of consciousness that might be called superconsciousness; and manifestation at this level is more concrete than it is in the Archetypal World. It is best thought of as the world where the patterns of the Archetypal World begin to take on shape.

Yetzirah, the third of the four worlds, is called the Formative World, and is the level of normal consciousness, although it can be said to include sub-conscious levels. Yetzirah, as its name implies, is the place of actual formation of things.

Assiah, the last of the Four Worlds represents the material world, and it is in this world that the various Planetary attributions listed on the Table on page 238 apply.

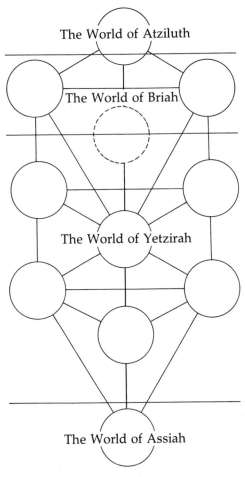

The World of Atziluth

The World of Briah

The World of Yetzirah

The World of Assiah

The Four Worlds

Unfortunately, the concept of the four worlds is not quite as simplistic as it would appear to be from the short description given above, for in point of fact, *every Sephira exists in all four worlds* — and all four worlds exist in every Sephira.

Perhaps the easiest way to deal with this very complex concept is to recognize the Four Worlds for what they are — separate, but overlapping dimensions in time and space — and to imagine that there are *four* Trees, each one superimposed upon the next. When viewed in this way — which is still overly simplified — the creation of the cosmos through the Rings and the Tree as an expression of the being of the Eternal Force can be seen as a logical progression of events rather like the construction of a building, which commences from an idea in the mind of the architect, through the various stages of blueprints and plans, material gathering, building, and final completion.

The four Trees postulated above are distinguished one from the other by **colour**. Colour Scales apply to both the Major and Minor Paths of Wisdom and can be used as 'signposts' on the 'roadmap' of the Tree, for they represent the

Table of Colour Scales — The Sephiroth

Sephira	Atziluth – King Scale	Briah – Queen Scale	Yetzirah – Emperor Scale	Assiah – Empress Scale
KETHER	Brilliance	White Brilliance	White Brilliance	White flecked Gold
CHOKMAH	Blue	Grey	Mother of Pearl	White flecked Red, Blue and Yellow
BINAH	Crimson	Black	Dark Brown	Grey, flecked Pink
CHESED	Deep Violet	Blue	Deep Purple	Azure, flecked Yellow
GEBURAH	Orange	Scarlet	Bright Scarlet	Red, flecked Black
TIPARETH	Rose Pink	Golden Yellow	Salmon	Amber
NETSACH	Amber	Emerald	Greenish Yellow	Olive, flecked Gold
HOD	Violet	Orange	Russet	Yellowish Brown flecked White
YESOD	Indigo	Violet	Dark Purple	Citrine, flecked Azure
MALKUTH	Yellow	Citrine, Olive, Russet and Black	Citrine, Olive, Russet and Black flecked Gold	Black, rayed Yellow

Table of Colour Scales — The Minor Paths

Path	Atziluth – King Scale	Briah – Queen Scale	Yetzirah – Emperor Scale	Assiah – Empress Scale
THE FOOL	Bright Pale Yellow	Sky Blue	Blue Emerald Green	Emerald flecked Gold
THE MAGICIAN	Yellow	Purple	Grey	Indigo, rayed Violet
THE PAPESS	Blue	Silver	Cold Pale Blue	Silver, rayed Sky Blue

THE EMPRESS	Emerald Green	Sky Blue	Early Spring Green	Rose, rayed Spring Green
THE EMPEROR	Scarlet	Red	Brilliant Flame	Glowing Red
THE POPE	Red Orange	Deep Indigo	Deep Warm Olive	Rich Brown
THE LOVERS	Orange	Pale Mauve	New Leather Yellow	Reddish Grey
THE CHARIOT	Amber	Maroon	Bright Russet	Dark Greenish Brown
STRENGTH	Greenish Yellow	Deep Purple	Grey	Reddish Amber
THE HERMIT	Yellowish Green	Slate Grey	Green Grey	Plum
THE WHEEL OF FORTUNE	Violet	Blue	Rich Purple	Blue, rayed Yellow
JUSTICE	Emerald Green	Blue	Deep Blue Green	Pale Green
THE HANGED MAN	Deep Blue	Sea Green	Deep Olive	Mother of Pearl
DEATH	Green Blue	Dull Brown	Very Dark Brown	Indigo Brown
TEMPERANCE	Blue	Yellow	Green	Dark Blue
THE DEVIL	Indigo	Black	Blue Black	Dark Grey
THE TOWER	Scarlet	Red	Venetian Red	Red rayed Azure or Emerald
THE STAR	Violet	Sky Blue	Bluish Mauve	White, tinged Purple
THE MOON	Crimson	Buff flecked Silver	Pinkish Brown	Stone
THE SUN	Orange	Yellow Gold	Rich Amber	Amber, rayed Red
JUDGEMENT	Orange Scarlet	Vermilion	Scarlet, flecked Gold	Vermilion flecked Crimson and Emerald
THE WORLD	Indigo	Black	Blue Black	Black rayed Blue

different modes of consciousness inherent within each Sephira or Path, the force of which can be contacted by using the correct scale.

The Colour Scales are attributed to the four worlds as follows:

King Scale is assigned to the world of **Atziluth**
Queen Scale is assigned to the world of **Briah**
Emperor Scale is assigned to the world of **Yetzirah**
Empress Scale is assigned to the world of **Assiah**

As with everything else applicable to the Tree of Life, these Scales follow the normal rules of the Principle of Polarity. Thus — for the purposes of meditation — the Major Paths of Wisdom should be visualized in King Scale; while the Minor Paths of Wisdom should be visualized in Queen Scale.

A Table showing these Colour Scales appears on pages 208 to 209 as they apply to both the Major and Minor Paths, and as these were not assigned arbitrarily, and do not exist merely to 'pretty up' the Tree (or make your life more difficult), you should make every effort to learn them by heart. If you do not, you will not be able to use them properly, nor perceive their proper effects upon yourself. More seriously, you may end by visualizing the wrong colour which can have a very detrimental — not to say devastating — effect. So do, please, make an effort to learn these colours properly — and learn to *visualize* them properly too; otherwise you will be wasting your time. 'Sliding' down the Tree via the Lightning Flash, visualizing colours as you go, is a very good exercise in this respect — and on those days when you happen to get the whole thing off, brilliantly and faultlessly in one go, can have an exhilarating effect which leaves you feeling very pleased with yourself for the rest of the day.

There are, of course, other attributions pertaining to the four worlds quite aside from the Colour Scales, and — fortunately — the most important of these is both the easiest to remember and the key to all the others too, i.e.,

Yod is attributed to **Atziluth**
He is attributed to **Briah**
Vau is attributed to **Yetzirah**
He is attributed to **Assiah**

This attribution of the letters of the Divine Name or Tetragrammaton to the Four Worlds carries with it all the other attributions you have learned to date, for example,

He: Water: Cups: Scorpio, Cancer and Pisces are all attributable to
Briah

The train of thought thus commenced can be carried forward to include the planets having rulership of those three Signs of the Zodiac and the gods and goddesses — which are, you will remember, personifications of cosmic force — associated with those planets. This is, of course, extremely useful; particularly if it is used as a basis for planned meditation, for each individual symbol throws light upon, and leads into, the next, so that the realizations gained are cumulative and much more revealing than they would have been had the full 'set' of symbols not been used.

There is also associated with the four worlds four sets of Named Beings — Powers and Principalities, if you like. These sets of attributions run as follows:

God Name — Atziluth
Archangel — Briah
Order of Angels — Yetzirah
Mundane Chakrah — Assiah

There are, of course, forty of these, four to each Sephira; and these too ought to be learned by heart, for their proper use (allied with the visualization of the correctly associated colour) yields the sort of worthwhile results that cannot be achieved in any other way. This means, I'm afraid, that you are faced with the mental absorption of forty colours and forty names, all of which have to be tied up together in the correct order. No easy task, and, sadly, no easy way either. This is, however, a task you can put off (unless you are actually *anxious* to begin; in which case please do start now with my blessing!), at least until you arrive at the exercises for the chapter entitled: 'Using the System', which is a guide to using the Tree, where you will find suggested a sensible course of action in this regard. A representative list of Named Beings is incorporated into that chapter, too, as one of a set of Tables designed for handy reference. In the meantime, you should try to absorb as best you can the concept of the four worlds *and at least one set of colours* (starting with the World in Atziluth) as soon as you can, and two sets of exercises follow in the usual form to help you do this. You should complete the first exercise and read the second one before you go on to the Spread for this chapter. You can then complete the second exercise at your convenience.

Exercise 1

1. Which Sephiroth constitute the world of Yetzirah?............................
    ....,

2. Another name for Briah is...

3. The Physical World is called................ and contains.........Sephiroth.

4. The four worlds are usually called..

5. The four worlds are distinguished one from the other by........................
    ....

6. The Colour Scale assigned to the World of Atziluth is called.....................

7. There are.....colours to each Colour Scale.

8. For the purposes of meditation, the Colour Scales follow the usual rules of the Principle of Polarity. In practice, this means that the Major Paths of Wisdom should be visualized in...................Scale; while the Minor Paths of Wisdom should be visualized in..............Scale.

9. Show how the letters of the Divine Name are attributed to the four worlds:

    .... is attributed to ATZILUTH

    .... is attributed to BRIAH

    .... is attributed to YETZIRAH

    .... is attributed to ASSIAH

10. Write out all the attributions you can think of that apply to the world of Yetzirah...

11. There are four sets of Named Beings associated with the four worlds. How many names would therefore constitute a representative list for the whole Tree?...

12. The Three Veils of Negative Existence are also known as.........................

13. What is the name of the unnumbered Sephira?...................................

14. How many Minor Paths of Wisdom are there?....................................

15. By what name are the two outer Pillars of the Tree sometimes known?.......
    ....

16. The Three Pillars of the Tree of Life are known collectively as...................
    ....

17. The central Pillar of the Tree of Life represents the element of...................in the Universe.

18. The Pillar of..............is feminine. The Pillar of..............is masculine.

Exercise 2

Drawn below are the ten Sephiroth of the Tree of Life. Fill in:

a) The twenty-two Minor Paths of Wisdom;

b) The colours of the world of Atziluth as they relate to the Major Paths of Wisdom *only*;

c) The Path of the Lightning Flash;

d) The Three Veils of Negative Existence;

e) The names of all three Pillars;

f) The names and dividing points of all four worlds.

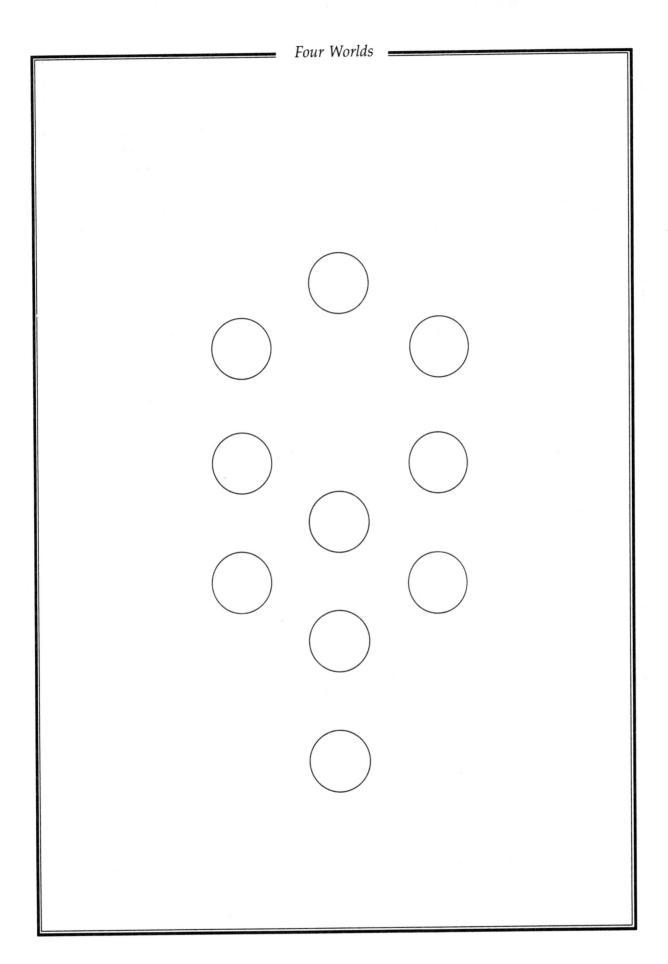

Instructions for the Tetragrammaton

1. Read and follow the instructions given in the Reader's Check List.

2. Place the Deck face down on the table, and ask the Querent to cut the cards in half, to the left.

3. Ask the Querent to cut the left-hand pile of the two piles thus created again to the left.

4. Ask the Querent to cut the right-hand pile of the two original piles to the right, so that you are left with four piles, all face down on the table, as per the first Spread on page 215.

5. Turn over the topmost card of each of those four piles, and read those cards having reference to the meanings given in the first Spread.

6. When you have completed the mini-reading, search each of the four piles for the Querent's Significator. *Do not* extract the Significator, or alter its position within the pile.

7. When you have found the Significator, discard the three piles that did not contain it, and lay out the pile which did contain the Significator in the pattern shown in the Second Spread, i.e., in lines from right to left, each line being of six cards; and from the bottom of the table to the top.

8. When you having finished dealing all the cards, look for the Significator. If the Significator is not surrounded by cards on all four sides, have the Querent choose another card at random from that portion of the Deck which you earlier discarded, and place that card so that the Significator is properly 'covered'.

9. Commence by reading the four cards surrounding the Significator. Then, and using the counting process, count your way through the layout, commencing with the Significator, i.e., the Significator will always have a numerical value of four, so the fourth card from the Significator will be the card you should next read. If that card has a numerical value of eight, the eighth card from that card should be the next card read, and so on.

10. When you arrive via the counting process at a card you have already read, turn your attention to the two columns at the right of the Spread. These columns represent the past, and should therefore be read before the four remaining columns.

11. The two central columns represent the present, and the last two columns, or those on the left of the table represent the future. They should,

therefore, obviously be read in that order.

12. Frequently, the Significator will not appear in the columns representing the present, but this is of no real significance.

First (Mini) Spread

Heh	Vau	Heh	Yod

Second (Real) Spread

6	5	4	3	2	1

The Tetragrammaton

17.

Twenty–Two Paths

The Minor Paths of Wisdom create a network of twenty-two interlocking pathways between the ten Sephiroth of the Tree of Life. The purpose of these pathways, as established forms of consciousness, is to harmonize and equilibrize the established forms of reality symbolized by the Sephiroth, thus maintaining a balance between the Major and Minor Paths of Wisdom in accordance with the Principle of Polarity.*

It is the cards of the Major Arcana that are associated with the Minor Paths of Wisdom. Unfortunately, while the positioning of Minor Arcana cards on the Tree of Life is straightforward and easy to follow and memorize, the positioning of Major Arcana cards is not.

As you will recall, Minor Arcana cards are placed on the Tree according to *face number* and following the Path of the Lightning Flash *down* the Tree:

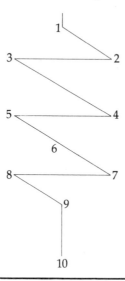

---

* Major Paths are considered to be masculine and positive (King Scale) to Minor Paths for the purposes of meditation.

Major Arcana cards, on the other hand, are placed according to *Key Number* (which does *not* appear on the face of the card), and follow a bewildering and snake-like course *up* the Tree that is usually represented by a picture of an actual snake, the coils of which are entwined about the Sephiroth and Paths, so:

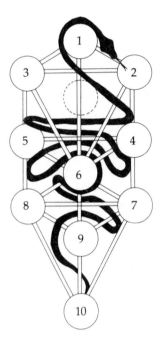

— this despite the fact that numeration commences with Path Number 11 at the top of the Tree:

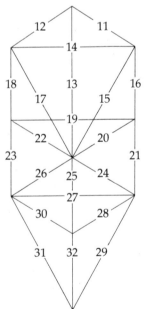

The logic of the numeration of the Key Numbers should be quite apparent, the numbers 1 through 10 having been already allotted to the Sephiroth.

Most courses of occult development (but not all) advocate commencement of work at the tail of the snake (Path 32), but it is quite possible — and in some ways easier — to commence work with Path number 11 and work downwards. From whichever direction work is commenced, however, some difficulty is bound to arise due to long-standing differences of opinion as to the proper placement of two pairs of the Major Arcana cards on the Minor Paths of Wisdom (i.e., Justice and Strength; The Emperor and The Star) and as to the placement of the first of these two pairs (i.e., Justice and Strength) within the Tarot Deck. The placement of all four cards on the Tree as shown in the diagram at the foot of page 221 is per the rules for their order laid down by the Hermetic Order of the Golden Dawn.

In the same way, and following the same rules of order, the cards Strength and Justice have for the purposes of this book been numbered 8 and 11 respectively. These two cards, however, were originally transposed as to face number, i.e., Justice was card number 8; while Strength was card number 11, and both cards appear bearing these face numbers in the Marseilles Deck and in Levi's book *Dogme et Ritual de La Haute Magic*; where, incidentally, the Hebrew letters — and consequently the Key Numbers of the Tarot Cards — also differ completely from the system later developed by the Golden Dawn.

Eliphas Levi discovered the apparent link between the Hebrew letters (which were already associated with the Tree of Life at that time) and the Tarot Deck; but he attributed the letter 'Shin' to the Card 'The Fool', thus placing this card between 'Judgement' and 'The Universe'. At the same time, however, he retained the original face number of the card — 'O' — and there is therefore some question as to whether his published attributions accurately reflect his private beliefs.

It is not at all unlikely that they did not. There is quite a lot of deliberately misleading and erroneous information to be found in occult literature due to the oaths demanded of the authors concerned by the various esoteric Orders to which they belonged. In any event, the members of the Golden Dawn accepted Levi's premise of a Tree/Letter/Card link, but rejected his published arrangement and rearranged the cards and letters into the order shown on the diagram at the foot of page 221.

Because of the changed position of the card 'The Fool' — which was moved to its present position on Path number 11 and allotted the letter 'Aleph' — all the Tarot card/Hebrew letter attributions save that of the Universe (Tau) changed too.

The new arrangement proved much more logical and satisfactory than the old; save only that if the cards were placed on the Tree according to their traditional sequence (i.e., Justice as card number 8, and Strength as card number 11), card number 8, Justice, fell upon the 19th Path (Astrological sign Leo), while card number 11, Strength, fell upon the 22nd Path (Astrological sign Libra). This was obviously incorrect; and consequently the positions of these cards were transposed — both on the Tree *and within the Deck*.

This latter transposition — with the consequent alteration of face number — was unnecessary and unfortunate, since it disturbed the integrity of the Deck as an entity complete unto itself, and ignored the esoteric import of its face numbering system. Whether the persons concerned in the transposition of these cards were unaware of the importance of the face numbering system to the Deck, or simply ignored it as a factor unimportant to their own purposes, is not known.

Older Decks of course, still adhere to the original (insofar as it is possible to refer to any modern Deck as 'original') — and correct — system of numeration, but most modern Decks (the Mandragora Press Deck being the only exception to spring to mind) were designed either by members of the Golden Dawn or their students, and consequently follow the system designed by that Order.

Cards number 4 and 17, (the Emperor and the Star respectively) have been transposed in some systems from the positions shown on the diagram at the foot of page 221, but have retained their original face numbers. The new positioning of these cards on the Minor Paths of Wisdom is shown on the diagram at the top of page 221.

These changes are the result of the work of Aleister Crowley, in whose book *Liber Regis — The Book of the Law*, there appears the all-important phrase:

'All these old letters of my book are right, but Tzaddi is not the Star.'

As you will see, if you look on the diagram at the foot of page 221, Tzaddi is the letter associated with the 28th Path; the traditionally allotted Major Arcana card being the Star; and the phrase referred to above, by casting doubt on this allocation, caused a considerable problem for everyone — including Crowley himself, who wrestled with it for some years before coming up with an answer. This he achieved by placing the signs of the zodiac upon the glyph of the Moebius ribbon, so:

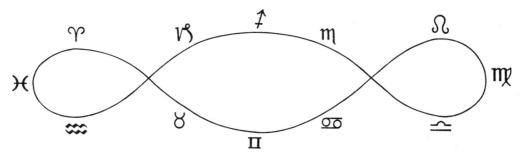

an arrangement which counterchanges two pairs of the signs, i.e., Leo and Libra; Aries and Aquarius.

The Moebius arrangement does not change the Astrological attributions of the Tarot Cards; thus ratifying the original arbitrary transposition of the cards Justice and Strength — at least on the Tree — and providing a reliable authority for the further transposition of the cards the Emperor and the Star at one and the same time.

Only one further problem arose in connection with the proposed transposition of these two latter cards; and this lay in the obvious Aries symbolism that still appears on most versions of the card 'the Emperor'. A very little research, however, shows that this symbolism is of comparatively recent date, and does not appear in pre-Golden Dawn Decks.

The transposition of the Emperor and the Star — along with the original transposition of Justice and Strength — is therefore nowadays almost wholly accepted, newer books (e.g. Gareth Knight's *A Practical Guide to Qabalistic Symbolism*) representing the Minor Paths as per the diagram at the top of page 221.

The difference of opinion discussed above — along with others less 'famous' but equally current — in no way compromise the system as a whole; but they do mean that it must be approached with an open mind rather than with an attitude of slavish obedience to tradition. The proper — and scientific — thing to do is to commence with the orthodox system and work with it until you are familiar with it. You can then go on to experiment with other systems (and they all have their adherents) until you either find the one which suits you best — or come up with a completely new one of your own; for it is more important to treat the Qabalah as a *living system* which is susceptible to change rather than to hold to a variation of that system with which you find you cannot wholly agree, simply because various authorities say you should. Before you do anything else, of course, you are faced with the not very exciting task of learning the traditional placement of the Major Arcana cards on the Minor Paths of Wisdom, *and the Colour Scales that go with them*, which latter are listed on pages 208 and 209. There are a good many more than forty of these this time, of course, and I would stress that before you attempt this exercise you should make sure that you are absolutely up to date with the rest of your work. To avoid any possible confusion, you should not start work on the Colour Scales and cards of the Minor Paths before you have the Colour Scales and other information relating to the Sephiroth absolutely right.

The exercise which follows is designed to help you get cards and Colour Scales right — and I'm afraid it will take you some time to get through it if you attempt it all in one go. This, however, is the last of the real 'learning exercises' to come your way, and is best approached with the practice exercises of the later chapters of this book; so you need not try to absorb it all at once — although you should, of course, read through it once before going on to the next chapter.

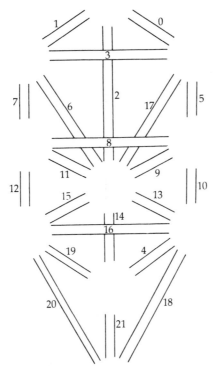

The Tarot Cards placed on the Tree by Face Number

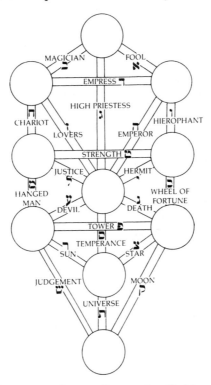

The Tarot Cards arranged according to the Golden Dawn system

Instructions for the Ladder Spread

1. Place the Significator at the bottom of the table. If you are using a Deck where Significators face to the right or left of the card, ascertain which way the Significator faces. If it faces to the left, place it to the lower right of the table. If it faces to the right, place it to the lower left of the table.

2. After following the instructions given in the Reader's Check List, lay out the cards as per the diagram opposite until you have exhausted the entire Deck.

3. Cards should then be read commencing at the Significator and climbing all the way to the very top of the ladder. The last card represents the eventual outcome of the divination.

This is one of the most difficult Spreads you can ever undertake. Obviously five timing cards will appear somewhere in the Spread, and you should take particular note of these, because they will be your only hint as to what is past, what is present, and what is future. Otherwise, the way to approach the Spread is to treat it exactly as you would a fantasy play. *Do not* attempt to develop a 'story line' in your head before you commence; because this will confuse you. The thing to aim for here is total spontaneity. Do not think about what you are saying, and try to develop an easy — even a monotonous — flow of speech.

Before commencing the reading, ask your Querent to defer any questions he may have until you come to the end of the reading. You should provide him with a pen and paper, if necessary, to write down any questions as may occur to him while you are speaking. The reason for this is that any interruption will disturb your train of thought and halt the easy flow of speech which is the ideal psychic reading. Once interrupted, that natural flow is often gone forever, which is frustrating for you and leads to a less satisfactory reading for your Querent, and you should stress this fact to your client before you begin.

When your Querent does begin to ask his questions *do not look at the reading again to try to discover the point from whence that question arose.* You will find that the answer to his question rises naturally to your tongue — and it should fall from your tongue just as naturally. Do not intellectualize. Above all *do not think*. Thought is conscious — and often erroneous. The answer that arises naturally from the subconscious is what is required here — and in every other reading — for it is rarely erroneous.

This is a real Tarot Reader's Spread — and it is what you have been aiming for. Try to do it well, and try to do it persistently until you manage it. You will find it well worth while, for a successful ladder reading is an achievement of which one might be justly proud.

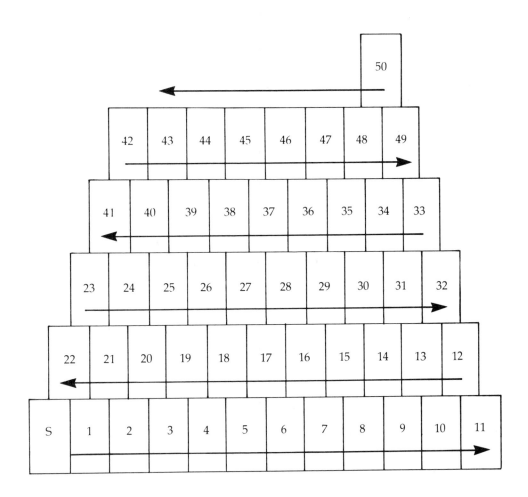

The Ladder Spread

Exercise 1

1. Take out the permanent mobile you made in the exercise to Chapter 13, and check it carefully to make sure that you constructed it correctly.

2. When you have completed this checking process, take out the 22 cards of the Major Arcana and set them apart from the rest of your Deck.

3. Turn to the diagram on page 221, and following that diagram carefully, peg your Tarot cards to your mobile with clothes pegs or paper clips.

4. Turn to the diagram on page 217 which shows the allocation of the Tarot cards to the Tree of Life by *Path Number*.

5. Take a sheet of paper and cut or tear it into 22 small squares. Write the number 11 through 22 inclusive on the squares.

6. Spend five minutes memorizing the diagram on page 217 and then, *without looking at it again*, try to place all 22 squares of paper in the correct places on the Tree. *Remember*, the 22 squares of papers represent Key Numbers, and although Key Numbers do not appear on the face of the cards — which are now pinned up before you in their correct places — you should remember which Key Number relates to which card from the sections dealing with divinatory meanings.

7. Work on the exercise for 20 minutes, and then check your results against the diagram.

8. If you are up to date with your work, you should be able to complete this exercise satisfactorily. If you cannot complete it satisfactorily, you should go on practising with the exercise day by day until you can — at which point you should take the cards down from the Tree, mix them up, and try to put them back. Because this exercise is designed to teach you to label the Paths by Key Number satisfactorily, you should, if you know your Key Number/Tarot Card link ups, be able to place the cards satisfactorily once you have learned the placing of the Key Numbers.

Exercise 2

Learning the Colour Scales is by no means an easy task, and one of the best ways to get over this is to construct a **Mnemonic** to help you remember what goes where.

Your Mnemonic should be a sentence that is constructed in such a way as to either:

a) Include all the colours of a given list; or

b) Hint at those colours via the first letter of every word of the sentence.

For example, the sentence below is a mnemonic for the Colour Scales of the ten Major Paths of Wisdom in King Scale.

Brilliant Bluebirds with **crimson** beaks and **deep violet** tails live in **orange** groves full of **pink** blossom and **amber** fruit under a **violet** and **indigo** sky and preen in the **yellow** sun.

The above sentence contains all the actual colours of the scale referred to, and — if you know the order of the Sephiroth — will show you what belongs where insofar as that scale is concerned. Naturally, a sentence for this purpose ought to be as memorable as possible, so it is much better to construct one of your own rather than using one constructed by someone else.

As an exercise for this chapter, you should construct a sentence of your own, for any Colour Scale you like (sentences for Minor Paths will obviously be much longer, and are in fact more difficult, so you are better sticking to

Major Paths for the moment) *that you have not already learned*. When you have constructed your sentence, leave it before you for the remainder of the evening, and read it over again before you go to bed. You should then not look at your sentence for a week. If, at the end of the week, you can remember the sentence, you may put it to the acid test — write it out as I have written out the example above, and then write the names of the Sephiroth over the top of the appropriate colours. If you find that your mnemonic has worked, then you should keep it, for it is obviously a good one; and at this point you can go to construct another. If it has *not* worked, then I'm afraid your mnemonic has proved a failure — which simply means that you will have to construct another!

18.

Using the System

When combined and unified as they are in the Western Tradition, the Tarot and the Tree form a route to mystical illumination and magical power. There are two ways to travel that route — the **mystical** and the **occult** way; and two ways to use the system — **actively** and **passively**.

The occult way is called 'The Way of the Serpent'. This involves passing along all twenty-two Paths of the Tree in the order shown on the diagram at the foot of page 221.

The mystic way is called 'The Path of the Arrow'. This follows the straight route provided by the Middle Pillar; but because the Middle Pillar is also the Pillar of Consciousness, and is thus a synthesis of the Tree as a whole, the traveller on this path experiences all twenty-two paths, just as the traveller on the Way of the Serpent does.

Both the Way of the Serpent and the Path of the Arrow are a means of achieving union with the Godhead in Kether. Neither route is better, nor easier, nor more ethical than the other; and choice of route is in any event not one that can be made on an intellectual level, or even at all; for one does not simply sit down and decide to be a mystic or an occultist. One either is, or is not, an occultist; just as one is, or is not, a mystic, and the natural propensity for either path that is inherent in every individual will manifest itself once the work is commenced.

Insofar as both occultist and mystic are concerned, however, following the chosen route as it is delineated by the Tree will in any event at first consist purely of meditation, and that meditation must commence with the Sephiroth and the manner of their manifestation. Planned meditation on the Tree of Life should therefore follow a structured pattern, as follows:

The first phase of the work should concentrate on the Unmanifest, the concretion of Kether, and the Sephiroth as individual entities, commencing with Kether, the First Manifest, and progressing, in an orderly fashion down the Tree of Life to Malkuth. It involves visualizing first the Unmanifest, and then each individual sphere in turn while using the correct Colour Scale and repeating/vibrating the appropriate Archangelic name. Because use of the correct Colour Scale and repetition/vibration of the 'name' constitutes an evocation of an aspect of the force of the Sephira involved, cumulative realizations as to the nature of the Sephira as a whole will naturally result.

When each of the Sephira has been dealt with singularly, work should commence on 'pairs' of Sephira, since, in reality, each Sephira emanates from its predecessor (so that Kether should be examined in conjunction with the Unmanifest and the Three Veils of Negative Existence from whence it emanates) and therefore cannot be satisfactorily examined entirely on its own merits. Thereafter, the work should continue with an examination of the Sephiroth as triads, beginning, of course, with the Superiors, or the Superior Triangle, and proceeding through visualization of the 'Four Worlds' aspect of the Tree — which is particularly important, in that it illustrates the otherwise inexplicable reasons for the gulfs that exist on the Tree and which impede the free passage of consciousness up and down it.

Work on the Sephiroth, the means of their manifestation, and their operation singularly and in concert is much simpler — and much less psychologically disturbing — than working the Minor Paths of Wisdom; for the realizations obtained by this sort of meditation are more universal, and less personal, the general result being a new way of looking at the workings of the unseen forces behind the mundane. This preliminary phase of the work is therefore usually exhilarating, enlightening, and comparatively painless. Moreover, because the Sephiroth represent the 'form concepts' of the duality that permits manifestation, work with them will ensure that a general understading of the realities of the system is achieved before any attempt is made to fathom its more subtle workings.

It is important, of course, not to 'stray' mentally during the course of meditation described above, and so all four of the Colour Scales relating to any given Sephira must be learned before meditation commences. Additionally, the other attributions of the Sephira concerned must be absorbed, one by one, before work is commenced, because these 'facts' are used in conjunction with 'starter phrases' as a basis for the exercise; and allow personal 'realizations' to be checked against traditional ones. This does not mean, of course, that any personal 'realization' gained in meditation that does not 'fit' the general run of attributions is absolutely and categorically wrong; but it does mean that these 'realizations' ought to be checked again by further meditation to ensure that interpretation of the 'realizations' gained is as unbiased as possible by personal preferences, traits and mores.

An exercise for the first phase of the work appears at the end of this chapter, together with a Chart giving short explanations of each Sephira, several 'starter phrases' and other relevant information. When you have worked your way through that exercise it will be up to you to construct a further series of exercises for yourself to complete the 'first phase series' of exercises. Ideas for such exercises can be culled from the books included on the 'Essential Book List' which appears at the end of this book.

Practice with such exercises will result, by the time the preliminary work on the Sephira has been completed, in the Colour Scales and 'names' becoming totally familiar and memorable, so that no real effort need be made to memorize the whole Tree in one go before commencing any meditation work at all.

Once work on the Sephiroth both individually and generally is underway — one cannot say completed, because of course it is never completed — and a very general understanding of the various spheres has been achieved, meditation work on the other Paths may safely be commenced.

Work on these Paths usually commences at Path number 11 and for the purposes of this book follows the Way of the Serpent *down* the Tree.

There are two kinds of meditation exercise native to the Western Esoteric Tradition insofar as it relates to the Minor Paths of Wisdom: **active** and **passive** Pathworking.

Passive Pathworking is a self-catered trip down the Path of your choice; a sort of 'cheap day return' scout-around affair that one can afford to take often. The purpose of such 'trips' is to observe the sights — and one's own reactions to them — on a gradual basis. Passive Pathworking involves first visualizing the proposed sphere of departure in King Scale; then stepping out onto and travelling along the chosen Path itself, which must be visualized in Queen Scale; and then visualizing (again in King Scale) and entering the sphere conjoining the other end of the Path.

In the case of Path number 11, this would mean commencing in Kether (King Scale — Brilliance); travelling the Path (Queen Scale — Eggshell Blue); and emerging in Chokmah (King Scale — Blue) while holding in one's head all the relevant information as to the states of consciousness and being represented by two Sephira and a Minor Path — this as well as experiencing and remembering the scenes and symbols arising in consciousness whilst travelling.

In this latter regard, there are, of course, many symbols associated with both the Major and Minor Paths of Wisdom, and many books which describe and explain these symbols in considerable detail. For the time being, however, you will be best employed in utilizing only the information set out in this book and the symbols of the Tarot — symbols with which you should, by now, be quite familiar — until such time as you have acclimatized yourself generally to the work, at which time you should graduate to Gareth Knight's *A Complete Guide to Qabalistic Symbolism* and Dolores Ashcroft-Nowicki's *The Shining Paths*.

The effects of Passive Pathworking are usually cumulative, but slow in coming, i.e., the psychological impact is 'cushioned' and rarely too uncomfortable or even immediately noticeable.

Active Pathworking, on the other hand, is very different. It is first class travel; literally a guided tour, for in this sort of Pathworking, another person 'guides' one along a single Path, using his or her voice and sometimes music and other sound effects to deliberately draw forth the appropriate psychological reactions.

Along the way, the 'guide' will point out sights so that nothing of importance is missed; and will present, one by one, experiences that then must be experienced because they cannot be avoided — as they often can on a self-catered trip.

The effects of Active Pathworking are far from slow in coming, because the very essence of what the Path has to offer is presented in one large — and very often psychologically indigestible — lump. At the same time, and because the immediate psychological impact is so great, it often takes some considerable time for those effects to wear off. Consequently, Active Pathworkings are for people who have completed all the preliminary work on the Sephiroth satisfactorily and who have thereafter taken self-catered trips on the Minor Paths of Wisdom for fairly long periods of time. *There is no way round this.* There are some taped guided Pathworkings on the market today, and these can be very useful, because they speed up one's progress so; but beginning one's career with these tapes is the psychological equivalent of attempting to run before one can crawl along; and you would do better *not* to seek them out until you have achieved some sort of psychological balance — however precarious.

The last exercise given at the end of this chapter is designed to allow you to experience guided Pathworking safely, and was purpose-written for you by Dolores Ashcroft-Nowicki, whose book *The Shining Paths* details pathworkings for all twenty-two paths of the Tree of Life, and who has personally pioneered public guided Pathworking. You are asked to follow the instructions for this exercise very carefully.

As a last point, and before you commence to use what you have learned, I would point out that although the 'map' formed by the Tarot/Tree system is marked, sign-posted and well travelled, it is not fail-safe unless it is used properly; and using the map properly means learning the route before you set out.

If, for instance, you do not know your Colour Scales as they apply to the Sephiroth, you will not be able to commence work at all, for you will never find the Gateway to the Path in the first place.

If you do not know your Hebrew letter sufficiently well to make a recognizable picture of it, you will not be able to commence visualizing the Path of your choice properly; for that letter is an integral part of the Gateway to the Path.

If you do not know your 'named beings' then you risk being turned back at the Gate of the Path by the individual who acts as Porter there; for those 'names' are passwords — 'tickets' to the Inner Worlds.

If you do not know your Colour Scales as they apply to the Path you are using, you will not be able to use them with exactitude or complete your visualization work properly — and you will consequently be likely to get confusing or peculiar results which will be worthless and possibly disturbing to you.

If you cannot recall the shape of the applicable Hebrew letter of the Path you are using once you are actually on it, then you will not be able to check your whereabouts, or to test any of the symbols, figures and situations of the Path with which you may find yourself confronted; for the letter is in this respect your lodestone and compass and a powerful weapon against possible deception.

If you do not know more or less what symbols to use or expect to see along the way, you will not be able to read the sign-posts as they appear; and you will risk getting lost or confused.

It is certainly unnecessary to learn the whole Tree by heart before you commence work on it, but it is *very* important that you know all there is to know about the small portion that you do intend working with — and you should find that you do know the whole Tree by heart once you have worked your way through it several times. Until then, however, please gather together the mental necessities of your trip before you travel, just as you would have the physical necessities of a trip ready to hand were you setting out on your annual holiday.

These mechanics aside, please be aware that there are rules to be observed on the Inner Planes; rules of behaviour, etiquette and conduct, and that these rules are much more stringent than their counterparts obtaining in the physical world, so you must take care to behave properly, and to observe the rules of the 'country' you are in while travelling.

The inhabitants of the Inner Planes are — on the whole — loving, wise, and very, very patient (they have, after all, all the time in the world), but they are also demanding, totally unbiased, sometimes not human as we understand the term, and no fonder of poor social behaviour than you are yourself. In addition, they have a habit of demanding the very best you can give.

It is worth remembering, too, that the Inner Planes are a place of *genuine* truth, and not truth as we are accustomed to use the word nor as we generally think of the concept. Consequently, there can be no facades there, such as we all usually build to shield ourselves from the world — or it from us.

* There you can't fool anybody — not even yourself.
* There a pretty face will not 'see you through' — as it very often will on the material level.
* There you can't 'get away' with anything, and it is a waste of time to try.

There, in fact, you will be seen for exactly what you are, however unpleasant what you are may be, and be accepted and loved, cared for and taught, as is, at face, and with warts.

So be graceful — be grateful.

Instructions for the Spread

1. Below, you will find a picture of a Spread. You will notice that it is simply a card layout, without any indication of how the Spread should be read; where the Significator should be placed; which cards indicate past, present and future; or how many cards there are at each placement. This is because this is an exercise which might best be called Design-a-Spread.

2. You should first decide, on looking at the layout, what sort of Spread you would like this to be. Should it be a Spread showing past, present, future? Or a Spread showing how your Querent feels, how people feel toward him, and what the situation really is? Should it cover one month, three months, six months, a year? What *kind* of Spread is this?

3. Having decided what sort of Spread it is you want, you should then decide how many cards should be in each place. One? Three? How many, and where? Should there be one card in the first pile, and four in the last? How many?

4. What about your Significator? Are you going to find this card before the reading? Read without a Significator? Search through piles for a Significator? What?

1	2	3
4	5	6
7	8	9
10	11	12
13	14	15
16	17	18
19	20	21

Note: Numbers refer only to card placements. They are not indicators of any kind.

Design-a-Spread

Instructions for the Three Fans Spread

1. Read and follow the instructions given in the Reader's Check List.

2. Shuffle and deal the entire Deck into three heaps of 26 cards each as per the diagram opposite.

3. Remove the heap marked 'B' on the diagram and keep it aside.

4. Shuffle the remains of heaps 'A' and 'C' back together again.

5. Deal the newly shuffled portion of the Deck into three further heaps. You will have one card extra. Keep it aside. Do not mix it up with the heap 'B' that you have already kept aside.

6. Remove the central heap of the three heaps you have before you. Place this new heap 'B' to the right of the original heap 'B'. Do not mix these two heaps.

7. Reshuffle the remainder of the Deck and mix in the extra card left over from the last deal. Deal the newly shuffled portion of the Deck into three heaps of 11 cards each. You will have two extra cards left over. Remove these two cards and set them aside.

8. Remove the central heap of the three newly made piles and place it to the right of the two 'B' heaps that you have already set aside.

9. Discard the remaining 'A' and 'C' heaps together with the two extra cards left over from the last shuffle.

10. Turn your attention to the three heaps you have extracted from the Deck.

11. Take the first of these heaps, or that which contains 26 cards and is the result of the first shuffle, and lay it out as per diagram 'A' opposite. The resulting Spread should be fan shaped, and is commenced from the lower right-hand corner.

12. *Read these cards*. They refer to the psychological condition of the Querent *now* and in the near future.

13. Take the second of the 'B' heaps — which incidentally should contain 17 cards and lay them out under the first group and as per diagram 'B' opposite.

14. *Read these cards*. They represent the Querent's work or occupation and his thoughts about that subject specifically.

15. Lay out the remaining, and third heap 'B', which contains 11 cards as per diagram 'C' opposite.

16. *Read these cards*. They represent the material condition of the Querent, his home life, health and financial situation.

17. Seek out the Querent's Significator. If it does not appear in any one of the three 'fans' of cards, deal out the cards previously discarded in the shuffling process — in a fan shape and in the same way as the three previous 'fans' — and read the resulting spread carefully for majorities and subsidiary majorities, for if the Significator does not appear in any one of the three original fans, then there is a specific question not covered by these which may be answered (and in a very specific way) by the fourth 'fan'.

18. If the Significator appears in the three original 'fans', point number 17 may be omitted — it is not necessary to read the 'fan' in which the Significator appears all over again.

This is a very good Spread to use for an overall six month reading where the Querent has no specific questions — or at least none that he can immediately call to mind. The Spread will of course raise questions — and you may then use other, and more specific Spreads in order to answer them.

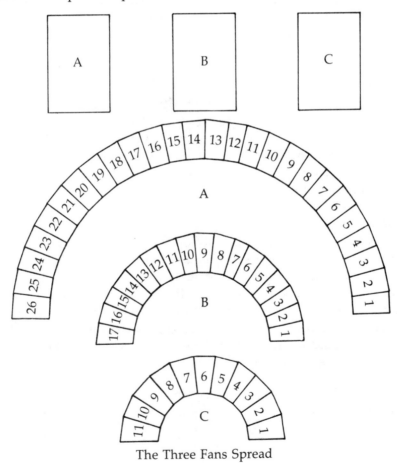

The Three Fans Spread

Notes to the Exercises

Meditation

When meditating upon the Sephiroth, try not to approach them from a purely mental viewpoint, for this results in rather arid meditation sessions. Instead, try to feel, as intensely as possible, all that the Sephiroth have to offer.

Additionally, it is important to *visualize* the various manifestations of the power of the Sephiroth, and the easiest way to do this is to imagine them as *cities*; places with character and inhabitants and all the usual appurtenances of cities. This is best achieved by reading carefully the table called 'General Attributions of the Sephiroth' and having reference to the Colour Charts for the Sephiroth given on page 208. This will help you to 'colour' your city as you visualize it.

Rhythmic Breathing

Rhythmic breathing is a rather important part of meditation after any system, for it improves the powers of relaxation.

The important thing to do with rhythmic breathing is to choose a rhythm (like breathe in, count 1, 2, 3, 4, breathe out) that is comfortable for you, and stick to it. The next thing is to remember *not to strain*. If you are not comfortable, you have more likely than not chosen the wrong rhythm, and should experiment to find the right one. Experimentation is the only formula for success with rhythmic breathing in any event, so it is worthwhile giving a little time and thought to it.

Don't worry either if you find that rhythmic breathing disturbs your meditations, for that disturbance does not usually continue for very long. You *will* find, of course, that you do think about your breathing initially, and you will probably find yourself counting as well; but there very quickly comes a time when you cease to think about breathing, cease counting, and find yourself doing it naturally.

Realizations

Realizations are fleeting things, and if you want to hold on to the interesting information you gain in meditation, you are going to have to write it down. However, writing meditations on odd scraps of paper which can be scattered hither and yon is not going to solve the problem of holding on to the realizations gained, so the best thing to do is to keep a Diary Record.

Diary records are best kept in Exercise Books that are used solely for the purpose, and should follow a set format. The format given below is the one most commonly used, and you could not do better than to follow it.

Meditation Subject   Date:
(Always write down your 'Starter Phrase'.   Time: *
Realizations without a Starter Phrase can be a   Place: *
little bit confusing.)
Realizations:

Exercise 1:
The Ten Sephiroth

1. Read this exercise through once completely, and make sure that you understand all the instructions, and can recall the 'Starter Phrase' and the scenes you are to visualize.

2. Turn to the Chart on page 238 and look up the entry there for the Sephira Kether. Write down and memorize that information.

3. Turn to the Chart on page 208 and look up the colour of the Sephira Kether in Queen Scale. Write down and memorize that information.

4. Turn to the Table on page 240 and look up the name of the Archangel of the Sephira Kether. Write down and memorize that information.

5. Turn to the Table on page 236 and look up the Starter Phrase allotted to the Sephira Kether. Write down and memorize that information.

6. Settle yourself comfortably in your armchair and complete the relaxation process described in Chapter 10 of this book. If you cannot remember the instructions for this process, turn to page 142, point 6, and refresh your memory.

7. Commence by visualizing a sphere around yourself in the King Scale colour allotted to the Sephira Kether.

8. When you have established your Sphere, vibrate the Archangelic name associated with the Sephira Kether, several times.

9. Vibration of the name should cause you to experience a sensation of incoming power and presence. When you feel you have achieved this feeling, to however mild a degree, commence *silent* repetition of the Starter Phrase.

10. Cease repeating the Starter Phrase. At this point you should try to see the Sephira in terms of a landscape, using the information given you in the Table on page 238. Eventually, pictures will begin to appear by themselves, and you should watch these carefully, and hold on to any thoughts that may pass through your mind.

---

* Optimum results will be obtained by standardizing the time and place of meditation.

Do not allow your thoughts to drift too far from the Starter Phrase; but if you find that you are seeing a landscape explore it carefully.

11. After 15 minutes or so, allow the meditatory state to recede. Do not try to retain this state for longer than 20 minutes, but allow yourself to come *gently* back to normal consciousness.

12. Open your eyes. Get up and stamp your feet. Write down your realizations (even if these consist only of a series of pictures or disjointed ideas)* before you forget them. Have a cup of tea or coffee.

You should continue this exercise for eleven days, dealing with one Sephira per day, and working *down* the Tree, ending in Malkuth. You should then spend a further ten days reversing the process, i.e., going *up* the Tree, commencing with Yesod and ending in Kether. You should then spend a further twenty days erecting the entire Tree in:

a) King Scale   (5 days)
b) Queen Scale   (5 days)
c) Emperor Scale (5 days)
d) Empress Scale (5 days)

This colour exercise should form the preface to a meditation session with the Sephira of your choice.

At the end of the twenty days, you should:

a) Know your Colour Scales very well indeed; and
b) Try to analyse why you chose to examine the Sephiroth you examined during the entire twenty day period.

Starter Phrases

Kether   The concept of other modes of existence is implicit in our philosophy and must always be borne in mind.

Chokmah   Rhythm is everywhere manifest in the Universe.

Binah   The Great Reservoir of space in which we live, move, and have our being.

D'aath   Here is total knowledge of beingness, life and creation.

Chesed   All spheres are Grails, each one a finer, more intangible version than the one before, but equally holy.

Geburah   Nothing in the vast expanse of space is dead.

---

* Sometimes, realizations do not make sense at the time, but come to make sense later. Sometimes, too, realizations are delayed, so be on the lookout for this for the next few days. If and when they do appear, write them down.

Tipareth	Within every man and woman is a force which directs and controls the course of life.
Netsach	In the one, can be found infinite diversity.
Hod	To think is to create. Thought is the DNA of all creation.
Yesod	Pressure on the soul plunges it into its own depths to seek the treasure within.
Malkuth	Mankind, collectively, is the soul of his planet.*

---

* Phrases are chosen from the works of Teilhard de Chardin, Israel Regardie, Dion Fortune, W.E. Butler and Dolores Ashcroft-Nowicki.

General Attributions of the Major Paths of Wisdom

Sephira	Vice/Virtue	Image	General
KETHER	Attainment	An ancient bearded king, in profile	Kether is also known as *Primum Mobile* or First Swirlings. It represents the beginning of things, and also the final ending of things; for this Sephira symbolizes that form of the Creator that is Alpha and Omega, the beginning and the ending. It indicates all first principles.
CHOKMAH	Devotion	Any father figure	To Chokmah is attributed the mundane Chakra **The Zodiac**, and the Sephira is sometimes called The Father. The Sephira as a whole can be regarded as a source of energy, and in particular masculine, life-giving energy. Its choir of Angels, **Wheels**, indicates the aspect of this Sephira which puts things in motion.
BINAH	Silence/Avarice	Any mother figure	To Binah is attributed the planet **Saturn**, which pertains to form, restriction and limitation. This Sephira is sometimes called The Great Mother, and it represents the feminine form-making principles as Chokmah represents the masculine force principles. This is the Sephira of birth, and consequently also of death.
D'AATH	Apathy or Inertia/ Detachment		D'aath is the Sephira of abstractions and absolute justice. It is to some extent associated with intuition; but revelation and inspiration are better words for this aspect of the Sephira. D'aath in its purest form has no symbolism at all, and there is consequently no magical image for this Sephira.
CHESED	Obedience/Cowardice and Pride, Hypocrisy, Gluttony and Tyranny	A mighty crowned and throned King	To Chesed is attributed the Planet **Jupiter**, and consequently it has to do with abundance, growth, organization and prosperity. Its virtue indicates co-operation with the codes of society. The Sephira is also connected with learning, and just law.

Sephira	Vice/Virtue	Image	General
GEBURAH	Energy and Courage/ Cruelty and Destruction	A mighty warrior in his chariot, crowned and armed	To Geburah is attributed the planet **Mars**, indicating action, initiative, critical judgement, energy and haste. Martial and surgical matters particularly fall under the dominance of this Sephira. The Sephira has the reputation of representing conflict and violence, but this is not really so — although it does govern change, and the overturning of the old for the new.
TIPARETH	Devotion/Pride and Vain-glory	A King, or a child, or a sacrificed god	To Tipareth is attributed **The Sun**, which is the centre of the solar system and the giver of all life. As you will recall, Tipareth is the centre of the Tree, and is the harmonizer of all manifestation. Under this Sephira fall all matters of healing, life, abundance and success, and this Sephira is the Christ Centre.
NETSACH	Unselfishness/Lust and Unchastity	A beautiful naked woman	**Venus** is the planet attributed to Netsach, and this is the sphere of right relationships. Under its dominance fall the emotions and the arts.
HOD	Truthfulness/Falsehood and Dishonesty	An androgyne	**Mercury** is the planet attributed to the Sephira, and under it come books, learning, communication, trade, commerce and the exchange of goods and ideas. Included in this list should be travel and contracts, the art of magic and thought in general.
YESOD	Independence/Idleness	A beautiful naked man	To Yesod is attributed **The Moon**, and so it has to do with rhythm, organic growth, fluctuation, tides and cyclic change. It also covers the subconscious, psychic and etheric, and biological functions of life.
MALKUTH	Discrimination/Avarice and Inertia	A young woman, crowned and throned	Malkuth is the centre for earth and material things. It is closely associated with Kether, of which it should be the material expression.

239

The Divine Names Attributed to the Sephiroth

KETHER	EHEIEH I am	METATRON	CHAYOTH HA QADESH Holy Living Creatures
CHOKMAH	JAH The Lord	RAZIEL	AUPHANIM Wheels
BINAH	JEHOVAH ELOHIM The Lord God	TZAPHKIEL	ARALIM Thrones
CHESED	EL God the Mighty One	TZADKIEL	CHASHMALIM Shining Ones
GEBURAH	ELOHIM GEBOR God of Battles	KAMAEL	SERAPHIM Fiery Serpents
TIPARETH	JEHOVAH ELOHIM VA D'AATH God made manifest in the sphere of the Mind	RAPHAEL	MELEKIM Kings
NETSACH	JEHOVAH TZABOATH Lord of Hosts	HANIEL	ELOHIM Gods
HOD	ELOHIM TZABOATH God of Hosts	MICHAEL	BENI ELOHIM Sons of God
YESOD	SHADDAI EL CHAI The Almighty Living God	GABRIEL	KERUBIM The Strong
MALKUTH	ADONAI HA ARETZ The Lord of Earth	SANDALPHON	ASHIM Souls of Fire

Exercise 2:
Passive Pathworking

The next two exercises to this Chapter are designed to highlight the differences between Active and Passive Pathworking, and to show how both these methods of working are best performed. You are asked to please follow the instructions carefully and to the letter. Please do not experiment with these exercises.

The first is an exercise in Passive Pathworking, and to complete it you must first find the Major Arcana card **The Fool**, and spend at least ten minutes 'mind's eye examining' this card.

When you have fixed the appearance of the card firmly in your mind, you should turn to the Table on page 121 and go through the same process with the letter **Aleph**. Look at this letter, and make sure that you can reproduce it, both in your mind and on paper.

Having completed this portion of the exercise, make sure that you know — and are able to visualize — the King Scale colours of the Sephiroth Kether and Chokmah. A Table giving these colours appears on page 208.

When you are quite sure that you have the items listed above fixed clearly in your mind, seat yourself in a supported position in your armchair, and then read the remainder of this exercise through once so that you remember what you are supposed to be doing before you commence the exercise itself.

1. You are going to imagine that you are standing in the Sephira Kether, and that this forms a circle of the appropriate colour about you.

    Before you, and inside the circle of Kether, stands a doorway. On the top of the doorway, engraved into the stone of the lintel, is the Hebrew letter Aleph.

2. When you have achieved a clear visualization of these things, step out through the doorway.

3. You will find that you are standing on a stone step. Before you stretches a crystal bridge, glittering in the sunshine. At the far side of the bridge, in the distance, you can see the circle of the Sephira Chokmah, which is your destination.

    Visualize this bridge, and the circle of Chokmah at the end of it, until it is quite clear.

4. Step out onto the bridge. It is quite safe and stable. It will not shatter under your feet.

5. Visualize before you, standing on the bridge, the Fool, looking just as he does in your Tarot card. Visualize him standing there. He is not moving. He is just an imaginary figure, standing on an imaginary bridge.

6. In your imagination, take a single step forward. Instantly, the Fool too will commence to move, and may gesture or even speak. This is perfectly

normal, and nothing to worry about.

7. Now, *listen, watch* and *follow* the Fool as he commences his journey. Observe any symbols or objects that may appear on the way. If you are apprehensive of any of these latter, superimpose over them the image of the letter Aleph. If they disappear, they do not belong on this Path and — obviously — if they remain, they do. Observe yourself, your thoughts and feelings, very carefully. Try to remember any conversations you may have.

8. Shortly, you will arrive at the end of the bridge, and will see, in the circle that represents the Sephira Chokmah, another portal, just like the one you left in Kether. Go through it.

9. See yourself standing in the circle of Chokmah. See the stone portal behind you, with the Hebrew letter engraved upon the lintel. See the circle gently fade away, then open your eyes and see your own familiar surroundings.

When you have completed this exercise, make a deliberate effort to 'come back to reality'. Write down your 'realizations'*; and stand up, move about, and get involved in your normal activities. **don't** remain sitting in your armchair, and **don't** drift off to sleep.

The journey of the Fool is generally a very pleasant one, and can improve the quality of your life, making you a more creative, purposeful and optimistic person. It is for these reasons, and because it rarely has any adverse effects at all, that it has been chosen for this and the following exercise. To ensure, however, that no ill effects befall you as a result of the guided journey that constitutes the next exercise, you should complete *this* exercise every day for six days before undertaking the Active Pathworking that follows.

Exercise 3:
Active Pathworking

For this exercise, you will need a tape recorder, and a blank tape.

To commence the exercise, you should read 'The Journey of the Fool' into your tape recorder, so that it is ready to play back when you need it. If you are working with a group, choose the person amongst you best fitted to read the exercise onto the tape. Try to put as much feeling into the reading as you possibly can.

When you have completed your tape, carry out the same preparations as for Exercise 2. Make sure you know your Colour Scales, and your Hebrew letter.

---

* Realizations often do not come at once; so what you will generally be writing as a result of this exercise is simply a history of what you have seen and experienced. You should look out, though, for realizations that come later — sometimes days later — and write these down as they occur.

When you are relaxed and ready, turn the tape you have made to 'play' and listen to it with your eyes closed. Build the images described on the tape with as much clarity and attention to detail as you can. It is important, for the purposes of this Pathworking that you *be* the Fool rather than simply follow him, for if you take on the actual persona of the main character in an active working, the results will be far greater than if you simply sit back and act the spectator.

When the tape stops, you should again follow the instructions given for the last exercise, i.e., wake up, write down your realizations, and go about your usual business. It is particularly important, when working with this exercise, not to remain in the state the exercise will induce.

Later, when you have grown accustomed to the exercise, you may experiment further with it, by adding music or other sound effects, but for the moment, taped speech is enough.

The Journey of the Fool

Allow the image of a door to form on the inner eye. Pay attention to detail. It is an oak door, with massive iron hinges and an ancient lock holding an intricately wrought key. Painted in black on the door is the Hebrew letter **Aleph**.

See the letter change to gold, and watch the colours flash, black and gold, black and gold, until your eye muscles relax and the inner vision takes over, making the scene vividly real.

The key turns in the lock — see it turn — and the door swings open — wide open — revealing a landscape of deep valleys and high mountains.

Still working in the inner realm of the mind, rise and go to the door, and look out upon the country beyond. Before you, leading from the doorway, is a well-trodden path. Waiting impatiently there is a dog, its tail waving joyously in welcome. Barking, it sets off down the path, looking back at you as if to encourage you to step over the threshold of this inner world. This you do, and follow the dog down into the valley.

All about you seems new and unexplored. You feel excited, as if you were at the beginning of a whole new way of being yourself. The air is slightly chilly but invigorating, and the sun shines overhead, reflecting on the snow-capped peaks. The dog is waiting for you, standing guard over something lying on the path. Bend down and look at it. It is a leather satchel closed with an intricate knot. A wooden staff still with a few buds on it lies beside the satchel. You pick them up and continue down into the valley.

The road leads to a clear stream of water, and you and the dog stop to drink. By the water is a rose bush with small white roses growing in profusion. The scent of the roses is strong and sweet. You pick one to take with you.

The road leads on through the valley towards the tallest of the mountains. As you walk along it, you see an eagle circling high above as if watching you. The land about you is rich and would take the plough well. You think of the rich gold of fields of corn and how it would look.

Now the road rises gently into the foothills, and you feel the need to rest. You take the satchel, and untie the knot closing it. It seems to be empty, but as you put your hand in, it closes around an object — a small loaf of bread and an apple. You eat and feel refreshed and ready to start your journey again.

The road gets rougher and more stony, and finally it is no longer a road, but a track, barely seen amongst the rocks and loose shale. The snow line is much nearer; the air is cold, and the wind is bitter. The dog stops and comes close to you, jumping up at the satchel as if to draw your attention to it. You stop and undo the knot, and put your hand inside. It seems impossible, but you draw from the small bag a warm cloak, and some stronger shoes.

With these, you make better progress up the mountain, for now you have started to climb in earnest.

The wind is very strong, and threatens to blow you off the track, although what track there is is now covered with snow. The way is almost impassable. The dog keeps ahead of you, forging a path with its own body to make it easier for you. In the sparse shelter of an overhanging rock, you stop to rest. In the satchel you find bread and a flask of wine. The bread you share with the dog, although it is scarcely enough to stay your own hunger. The wine warms you a little, but not nearly enough.

The dog beside you looks weary, and shivers with the cold. It is not as big as you had thought it to be, and its paws are frozen and bleeding where the sharp stones have cut through the pads.

You look up and see the summit very near now, and for the first time you wonder why you have taken this road, where you are going, and why. You try to remember where you have come from, but the memory is dim. All you know is an insatiable desire to go on, to follow where this path leads, to endure, and to conquer. You must go on. Rising, you pick up the dog and tuck its cold body into the folds of your cloak, take up the satchel and the staff that lies near it, and prepare to make a final effort to reach the top.

The extra weight of the dog seems to draw your strength very fast. There is a temptation to leave it behind to fend for itself, but the thought is quickly gone, for you are companions. The staff helps you to struggle up the last few feet, and with one last effort you reach the top.

You have not thought what you might expect to find here — more snow perhaps, or a path leading down the other side of the mountain? What you do not expect to find is a warm, sunny plateau.

The path appears clearly leading straight to the edge. There is no way down, except to go back the way you came. But that is unthinkable. You stand up, throwing off the cloak, releasing the dog, who runs about barking and enjoying the warmth. You sit down, and try to think about your journey and its meaning.

You have climbed up from the green valley, with just the company of a life-form for which you have taken responsibility, and which in turn has repaid you with affection and with help. You have dared to seek a way through adversity and struggle. You know you must go on. You know that you cannot turn back. From the satchel comes the heady scent of the rose you picked in the valley. You take it out, and its sweetness fills your senses as you breathe in the scented air. You know now that your way is forward. Your faith in your destiny is stronger than your fear of the edge of the plateau.

You walk to the edge, and look down. There is no valley below you, but only a deep blue void. You look up at the sun. The dog stands quietly beside you. Then you pick up the satchel and sling it over your shoulder, grasp the staff firmly in one hand and call to the dog. It leaps up barking and joins you as you both leap over the edge.

You spin gently, but whether downwards or outwards or upwards you do not know. You drift in the void for an endless time, conscious only of the satchel, the staff in your hand, and the presence of the dog. Then, even these things leave you, and you are alone, falling slowly into a half sleep, but carrying with you the memory of your journey.

You feel a slight bump, and find yourself in your chair looking out of an open door at a landscape of valleys and mountains.

Slowly, the door closes, and the key turns in the lock. See it turn. The letter Aleph on the door glows briefly, and then letter and door fade from your inner sight and you wake in your own physical world.

Written for *The Tarot Workbook,* by Dolores Ashcroft-Nowicki

19.

Moments of Truth

Always supposing that you have worked your way conscientiously through the preceding chapters, you are now moderately familiar with your Tarot Deck, and capable of reading several Spreads easily and with a satisfactory degree of accuracy. Your primary requirement at this point therefore is *practice* — and by practice I mean *real* readings for *real* Querents.

Whatever your reasons for deciding how to use the Tarot, the period of intensive practice you now face is a most necessary part of your development, and you should on no account delay or avoid it. Practice will consolidate all that you have learned to date, and serve to fix the new knowledge you have so painfully acquired firmly in your memory. It will give you the sort of insight into your cards that is an integral part of using them. Most importantly of all, it will give you the invaluable gift of practical experience.

Any readings you undertake at this time will of course lack the smooth and easy delivery that comes with years of practice; but they will be *adequate*, and — for the time being — adequate is the best you can hope to be.

You should read over the next few weeks as much and as often as you conveniently can, practising until your Tarot cards have become absolutely familiar; until you can lay out Spreads and choose Significators in your sleep; until you have mastered the mainly by-rote mechanics of meeting, greeting, listening, talking; and until your readings run smoothly from the arrival to the departure of your Querent. Until, in short, you are quite a bit better than just *adequate*. It will be a wearing process, but a useful and enlightening one.

This means that you must expand your reading orbit, and begin to deal with people who do not form part of your immediate circle and whose lives and circumstances are unknown to you. Happily, this is not at all hard to do, as anybody with the ability to read Tarot cards and a friendly and obliging disposition has what amounts to an infallible recipe for instant popularity. Even should you lack a large enough circle of acquaintances to provide you with sufficient free advertising and an adequate supply of guinea pigs, a simple notice something on the lines of 'New Tarot Reader Needs Practice —

Free Readings' tacked up in a public place* will bring you more than enough clients to fulfil your needs for the present. Before you leap out, cards in hand, however, and commence filling your telephone book with new and interesting names and addresses, there are one or two things you should think carefully about:

1. **Exploitation**

It is very easy for almost anyone to exploit new and inexperienced Tarot readers, simply because they are usually pretty pleased with themselves and anxious to display their new talents; but it is even easier for the Tarot reader to exploit the general public, sometimes in all innocence, and sometimes knowingly and with malice aforethought. *Don't*, therefore, be bullied into reading for large groups of people one after the other at the very beginning of your career, because this is bad for *you*; and *don't* be cajoled into a daily reading for anyone at all, because this is bad for *them*.

Reading large groups of people can be a debilitating and time-consuming process, as you will soon discover for yourself if you agree to read at a large party or charitable function. It is hard to do one's best under such circumstances. Time is always pressing; there are always people lounging about drinking and chatting and exuding impatience somewhere much too close at hand; and the atmosphere generally is far from the quiet and restful ideal. Eventually, you will be able to handle functions of this kind quite well, but for the moment you would do best to avoid them.

This means, I'm afraid, that you should also avoid being pressed into reading for whole parties of friends — and you inevitably will be so pressed immediately your interest in the Tarot becomes common knowledge. This pressure is less open than insidious, and can create certain social difficulties for you, since it is always difficult to render point blank refusal inoffensive. The best thing to do under these circumstances is to offer to read for your friends one by one at home, setting up proper appointments, and explaining your reasons for this carefully. In this way you will avoid giving offence and at the same time will create a situation that is better for your friends and much, much better for you. Tarot reading is fun; but reading away your evenings monotonously, working, literally, at what ought to be your social engagements, is *not* fun. In fact it very quickly becomes boring, and you will begin to develop a certain resentment at being cornered — very much as certain professional people are cornered — and forced to listen patiently to a catalogue of questions to which your various interrogators seriously and sincerely believe you to have a series of wise and farsighted answers.

---

* Obviously, if you advertise publicly, you must take steps to safeguard yourself. Always make sure that there is someone close at hand to help you if need be before you invite a total stranger into your house, and never agree to visit someone else's home unless you are at the very least acquainted with them or have been introduced through a reliable friend.

If you are not firm in resisting this sort of thing from the very beginning, there will inevitably come a day when you are going to be forced to *become* firm, and as this has been known to cause unpleasantness you are better off starting as you mean to go on. In the meantime, if you must take your harp to the party, make sure that you have arranged — in advance — to play. In this way you will be able to bring your host to some understanding of what is required by you — like a quiet area to work in, an adequate supply of refreshments (but *not* alcoholic refreshments for *you*, please), and a limited number of guests — to ensure that the evening goes off to everybody's satisfaction, and you will not be forever crawling away from your social engagements bored, resentful, and in an advanced state of exhaustion.

Don't consult the Tarot too often on behalf of any one individual — even if that individual happens to be you. In the first place, daily readings lack the significance and depth of readings spaced over long intervals, and quality of results declines drastically. More importantly, the Tarot (like any other divinatory tool) has a tendency to become a crutch for the weak and the vacillating, and the voice of absolute truth for the believer. *Neither of these things it can ever or should ever be.* Any disposition on the part of your Querents and friends to rely too heavily on you and your Tarot Deck — to telephone you, for instance, and ask your advice before completing some simple action — should be strongly discouraged from the outset, and you should not be slow to discover and check this trait in yourself. The results of an obsession with divination are never happy, and much time and many valuable opportunities can be lost by the individual who falls victim to one. Unfortunately, such obsessions are all too common, and are all too commonly encouraged — usually by unprincipled people who make large sums of money fostering and exploiting dependency in their clients. Making sure that such obsessions do not occur is one of your most important responsibilities as a reader, so remember: readings for a single individual should be spaced at least six months apart — preferably longer — and there should be *no* exceptions to this rule.

2. Opinions, Conclusions and Advice

It is your job as a reader to draw a sensible and accurate forecast picture securely based on your assessment of your client's past and present circumstances. It is *not* your job to form opinions, draw conclusions, or give advice — although you will very often be asked to do all three.

When you *are* asked to give an opinion or offer advice, and feel that you have something useful and concrete to offer your client, it is perfectly alright to go ahead and state your case, but you *must* disassociate these personal comments from the reading, and you *must* remind your Querent that as a layman with no training as a professional counsellor your advice is worth no more than anybody else's. The best way to perform this act of disassociation is to ask your Querent to wait for a few moments while you pack your cards away and make a cup of tea or coffee. This homely everyday activity will create a more informal and relaxed atmosphere and ensure that any comment you may make will be in no danger of being misconstrued.

I stress the importance of this act of disassociation because of the enormous power readers have over their clients — a power that is often underestimated by reader and Querent alike. You should at all times be aware that there are some individuals who are deeply impressionable or a prey to superstition, and modify your behaviour accordingly. Remember, *anything* you say to *anyone at all* in your persona of reader can take on an importance out of all proportion to your intention or its real worth. For the same reason, you should *never* read for children — they are much too easily influenced — or treat Tarot reading as a game or party piece. Tarot reading is *not* a game, and it can never qualify as something that can suitably be undertaken merely to pass away an evening. The words of a reader — even if they are totally inaccurate — are inclined to stick in the mind of a Querent (however sceptical and pragmatic an individual the Querent may be) with astonishing persistence and may actually influence his life. Try to bear this in mind, and approach your new interest in a consistently serious, responsible and adult manner.

3. Readers are People

But only when they are not being readers. You cannot afford, as a reader, to have personal preferences; likes or dislikes; religion or politics. A good reader is an Equal Opportunity Reader. He develops a high degree of detachment, is 'blind' to his clients' looks, lifestyle, politics, colour, religion, social standing, etc., — and consequently reads with a high degree of accuracy simply because his readings are not 'sieved', as it were, through a collander of personal experience and bigotry. It is not easy to 'forget yourself' in this way, and nobody ever achieves total detachment, but it is essential that you at least make a serious attempt at it.

It is essential too that you realize that as a reader you forfeit some of your rights as an ordinary person. You cannot, for instance, be late, or just not turn up, for a reading. You cannot be rude either, or disapproving, impatient, sarcastic and unkind. If your Querent behaves abominably (and some of them do) then you are within your rights to terminate the reading immediately, but this is the limit of your retaliatory powers. The bottom line is: if you cannot deal with the general public on a day-to-day basis without losing your head or your temper, then you cannot be a reader.

4. Querents Are People, Too

It is to your advantage to give generously of your time, patience and sympathy when reading, and to make your Querent feel comfortable and welcome in your house. A relaxed and happy Querent is a well-behaved Querent, and is, moreover, easier to read, so be thoughtful about your client's welfare and sensible about your approach.

Don't, for a start, indulge in ridiculous and theatrical atmospheric effects that may automatically bring what you are doing into ill repute, and frighten or disturb your Querents. Very few people can be at all comfortable in a room lit solely by candles, or so filled with the smoke and odour of cheap commercial incense that breathing is both difficult and unwise; and hardly anyone at all really wants to be confronted with a reader dressed as Omar the Tentmaker or so shrouded in exotic garments as to resemble a mobile oriental clotheshorse rather than a human being.

Time spent trying to be interesting in this way is time wasted. The Tarot doesn't need props — and neither does the average Querent, who, on the whole, quite likes to be able to see you, your house, and his hands in front of his face — so treat your Querent as you would any other guest, and leave stage management to the local amateur dramatic society. Be neat and well-groomed, and make sure your home is neat and well-groomed too. Don't keep your Querent waiting while you clear a space for him to sit down, and don't leave him clutching his coat — or sitting about perspiring in it — when you do seat him. Arrange your furniture comfortably beforehand, and take your client's coat away and hang it up immediately he arrives. If you have an animal in the house, enquire as to whether your Querent is allergic to it — or nervous of it. If he is, remove the animal to the kitchen for the duration. *Don't* put it in the bathroom. Readings can be surprisingly diuretic, particularly if they go on for more than an hour, and a client who is engrossed in a pressing physical need is neither happy nor comfortable. For the same reason, always offer your client a cup of tea or coffee. Most people expect to be offered something of the sort, and so put off getting anything on their way to see you. If something is then not offered they are forced to sit there, thirsty and miserable, until you release them. In the meantime, they are quite unable to participate fully in the reading because their attention is elsewhere.

Watch your Querent. Don't become so engrossed in what you are doing that you ignore your subject. Some people are unreasonably nervous of Tarot cards, or totally unfamiliar with them, so be alert for manifestations of discomfort or alarm. A Querent who is staring mesmerized and aghast at a Tarot picture that disturbs him is not listening to what you are saying, and may go away apprehensive as well as unenlightened. *Look* at your Querent periodically as you read, *be aware* of his reactions, and if necessary reassure him or change the tack of your reading. There is no need to upset your Querent by giving chapter and verse on a subject he finds distressing or distasteful.

Don't make hard and fast rules about the time you are prepared to spend on each reading. It is all very well to set a *general* time limit, but if your Querent is distressed or simply unwilling to leave, don't insist on sticking to it. The majority of Querents lead full and busy lives, are cheerful and polite, and come disposed to be pleased. Consequently they are easy to deal with and rarely take up more than an hour of your time. Unfortunately, however, not all Querents conform to this ideal, and you must be prepared to take the rough with the smooth. If your Querent is obviously suffering from desperate loneliness, or shows an acute need for human companionship, or bursts into tears immediately his or her feet are safely planted under your table, then you are going to have to spend as long as it takes to deal with the situation satisfactorily. You may miss a few dates and television programmes by adhering to this rule, but if you are not prepared to do at least that, then you shouldn't be reading at all. Remember, *sad* people — people who genuinely need your help and for whom you may very well be the court of last resort — are your real *raison d'être*, and it is they who make the whole process of reading Tarot for the public useful and worthwhile.

5. Quality of Reading

Quality of reading depends on two factors — you and your Querent. Some Querents are easy to read; others are not. All readers have 'good days' when quality of results is very high; all readers have 'off days' when quality of results can be very poor indeed. There is no discernible pattern behind either of these phenomena, but there is a golden rule to follow when dealing with them: *don't try to 'fluff' it*. If for any reason you feel you can't do a good job, *say so*.* Nobody is going to take you out and hang you for it; you can't help having an off day any more than your Querent can help being a bad subject for divination, but if you try to struggle on regardless of these drawbacks you will make bad worse and may get yourself a reputation as a charlatan. In the Tarot, as in everything else, honesty is by far and away the best policy.

6. Policy

Money as payment for services rendered by Tarot readers is a very vexed question, and one that is hotly debated in the field as a whole. Happily, it need not trouble you for at least a couple of years or more — it is going to take at least that long to make your readings worth a bent penny of anybody's money.

Don't charge regular fees until you are worth it, and when you are worth it, make sure your fees are reasonable and within the reach of everyone. Enormous fees (and, so far as I personally am concerned, *fixed* fees) are unethical.

7. What Next?

There are two alternatives available to people who want to continue the studies they commenced with this book. The first is to construct a curriculum of work and press on with it alone. The second is to seek out a group that offers a pre-packaged curriculum and some measure of supervision.

The first of these alternatives is not ideal. It is neither wise nor particularly

---

* But make sure that your subject understands *why*. If you turn people away without adequate explanation they may fall victim to dire fears and imaginings — primarily because this scenario has formed an integral part of the plot of a good many commercial horror films.

satisfying to work without check or supervision or the feedback that supervision generates; and, indeed, this situation sometimes leads to a compounding of an original and unsuspected error that would have been avoided had some measure of supervision been available. However, as this option is often the only feasible one, it must be seriously considered here.

People who opt for, or have no choice but to follow, this first alternative, must, of course, work from books; and although there are a multitude of books to choose from these days, not all of those available are immediately useful or 'essential books'. Because of the difficulties involved in identifying which book among an entire bookseller's stack of books might be termed 'essential' I have included a list of 'essential' books. This is not a very long list; but once you have read your way through it you will be much more capable of choosing 'essential' books along the lines of your own personal development than you are — in all likelihood, in any event — at this moment.

The second of the alternatives mentioned above, that of finding a group with which to work, is the ideal. It can be somewhat more expensive than working alone, for this alternative too, demands the purchase of books, and there is usually some additional charge to be taken into account for the purchase of lessons as well; but these are, on the whole, worthwhile and quite good value for money. Additionally, there is the advantage of having help and supervision to be taken into account.

Finding a group is the ideal way to progress, but it is often a difficult idea to put into practice, since organized groups who welcome new students are a bit thin on the ground these days. However, there are groups to be found, and they can be found via occult book shops, occult magazines, enquiry of the Director of the group the address of which appears at the end of this book, or by the purchase of Marion Green's book on groups.

Even if you are absolutely intent on finding a group, however, you should not cease work altogether while you concentrate on finding one; because that project might take you some time, and is in any event not something to be undertaken in a hurry. Instead, you should gather together your 'essential' library (which you will need in any case) and work with it by yourself for a while. Neither, incidentally — and this is very important — should you join the first group you come across that is prepared to accept you, simply because you fear that you will never find another. It is not true that any teaching is better than none at all — far from it — and quite often, when you are 'ready', a group will find you.

8. A Word of Warning

The occult in any form is not universally well thought of, and so must essentially remain a private affair. It is not a subject that one can with confidence introduce into general conversation, and an interest in it will not endear you to the corporate world at large. *Be careful.* Don't lose your promotion, or antagonize your workmates or neighbours by talking about it when neither time nor place is suitable. Remember that there are still some people who find the whole field abhorent, offensive or unnatural, and bear in mind that while the occult can be absorbing and exciting — and rewarding — it is not intended to replace ordinary life as a source of excitement or to become anyone's *sole* interest. Keep your sense of proportion, and learn to keep your own counsel — you will be the better an occultist for it.

'Essential' Reading

Ashcroft-Nowicki, D., *The Shining Paths* (Aquarian Press, 1983)

Avery, Kevin Quinn, *The Numbers of Life* (Doubleday, 1978)

Butler, W.E., *How to Develop Clairvoyance* (Aquarian Press, 1979)

Butler, W.E., *How to Develop Psychometry* (Aquarian Press, 1979)

Butler, W.E., *Introduction to Telepathy* (Aquarian Press, 1975)

Case, Paul Foster, *The Tarot* (Macoy Pub. Co., 1975)

Cirlot, J.E., *A Dictionary of Symbols* (Routledge, 1972)

Fortune, Dion, *The Mystical Qabalah* (Aquarian Press, 1935)

Fortune, Dion, *Psychic Self-Defence* (Aquarian Press, 1977)

Hope, Murry, *Practical Techniques of Psychic Self-Defence* (Aquarian Press, 1983)

Jung, C.J., *Man and His Symbols* (Pan Books, 1978)

Knight, Gareth, *A Practical Guide to Qabalistic Symbolism* (Helios, 1965)

Lüscher, Max, *Lüscher Colour Test* (Pan Books, 1972)

Marsden, R., *Psychic Experience for You* (Aquarian Press, 1983)

Regardie, Israel, *The Tree of Life* (Wieser, 1980)

Regardie, Israel, *A Garden of Pomegranates* (Llewellyn, 1978)

Roberts, R., *Tarot Revelations* (Roberts, 1979)

Emily Peach is a student of the Servants of the Light Association, which runs a postal course of instruction based on the works of W.E. Butler. This is a fully contacted school of the Western Mysteries and teaches a full curriculum of esoteric sciences. The work is under strict discipline and personal supervision.

The Servants of the Light Association can be contacted at:

P.O. Box 215
St. Helier
Jersey
Channel Islands
Great Britain

Index